A Thread of Gold

16|26.

(1990)
£3
6e
Inscribed.

A Thread of Gold

Journeys towards Reconciliation

*

Albert H. Friedlander

To Pierre:

whose writings I admire,
and with whom I share much.
In friendship
Albert

London
Oct 30, 1990

SCM PRESS LTD
London

TRINITY PRESS INTERNATIONAL
Philadelphia

Translated by John Bowden from the German
Ein Streifen Gold,
published 1989 by Christian Kaiser Verlag, Munich,
with revisions and additional English material by the author.

This edition first published 1990

SCM Press Ltd   Trinity Press International
26-30 Tottenham Road   3725 Chestnut Street
London N1 4BZ   Philadelphia PA 19104

British Library Cataloguing in Publication Data

Friedlander, Albert H. (Albert Hoschander) 1927–
A thread of gold: journeys towards reconciliation.
1. Jewish culture, history
I. Title   II. [Streifen gold. *English*]
909.04924

ISBN 0–334–02467–6

Library of Congress Cataloging-in-Publication Data

Friedlander, Albert H.
[Streifen Gold. English]
A thread of gold : journeys towards reconciliation/Albert H.
Friedlander.
p.   cm.
Translation of: Ein Streifen Gold.
'With revisions and additional English material by the
author'
–T.p. verso.
Includes index.
ISBN 0–334–02467–6 (pa)
1. Friedlander, Albert H.—Journeys—Germany.
2. Germans—Attitudes.   3. Judaism—Relations—
Christianity—1945–   4. Judaism—Relations—Christianity—
1945–   5. Reconciliation—Religious aspects—Judaism.
6. Rabbis—England—London—Biography.   7. London
(England)—Biography.   I. Title.
BM755.F698A313   1990
296'.0943'0904—dc20   90–39231

Phototypeset by Input Typesetting, London
and printed in Great Britain by
Clays Ltd, St Ives plc.

One day, after the destruction of the Temple, the disciples of the rabbis were walking with their pupils near the Temple. And they were weeping. 'When will redemption come?', they asked. Their teachers answered: 'The question always comes in the dark of night, when redemption seems impossible – it will never get light again. But then comes the dawn, first slowly, a white line on the horizon, and then, suddenly, a thread of gold. And with the first rays of the sun the darkness is banished. So it is with redemption. It begins slowly, almost imperceptibly, but then it comes faster and faster, and suddenly the whole world is in bright light.'

Sketch for a portrait of Rabbi Friedlander
R.B. Kitaj

For
Evelyn, Ariel, Michal,
Noam, Dorrit and Charles

Contents

Preface to the English Edition

The German text of this book reported my journeys towards dialogue and reconciliation within what was called East and West Germany in 1988 and 1989. We live in a different world now, and I have added reflections and encounters which have taken place in 1990. In the process I have discovered that the events of 1988 and 1989 take on an additional importance for me. In part, because they describe a world that no longer exists in that form, but has realized some of the hopes expressed by my East German friends in unexpected ways. In addition, I now recognize some of the signals given to me at an earlier time, and my obtuseness in not understanding the language of a people under oppression. To put it bluntly, I was blind, and my much more relaxed friends in East Germany have not hesitated to tell me so in my recent visits. But why should my past stupidity not be recorded in print? Why should this book be different from other books, particularly when it appears at a time of so much change that neither prophets nor pundits are to be trusted?

The preface also gives me the opportunity to thank John Bowden, my editor and translator. It was, I confess, a hard blow to my pride to be told that I should not translate my own book; after all, English is now my first language, and I make even more mistakes in German. John Bowden gently pointed out to me that authors who translate their books are like lawyers who plead their own case and have a fool for a client. Also, I would be tempted to write a different book – not the one he had chosen to publish. I accepted his wisdom, and his superb translation – and am grateful. I would like to think that the readers of this text will not hold him responsible for the contents, but will walk along with me on a journey midway between laughter and tears, but one which may yet move towards dawn, towards the first thread of gold on the horizon.

Albert H. Friedlander

London, Great Britain
June 1990

Introduction

Martin Buber's *The Way of Man* teaches that every journey to our fellow men and women is first a journey inwards, into our own existence. 'Rabbi Bunam taught: Our wise men say, "Seek peace in your place." You cannot seek peace elsewhere than within yourself, until you have found it there. The psalm says, "There is no peace in my bones because of my sin." Only when someone has found peace in himself can he go on to seek it throughout the world.'

The recognition of a turning point in one's own life and in the life of one's fellow men and women is an inner experience which ultimately brings us peace. We live in our own imperfection, and sin burns in our bones until it is overcome. This teaching of Buber's came to me through my encounter with the master, and perhaps it is also significant for my encounter with the Germans.

For decades I resented Martin Buber. Resentment ran in my bones like fire and was almost insuperable. In 1963, when I was a student chaplain at Columbia University in New York, I finally finished a translation of Leo Baeck's *This People: Jewish Existence*, which had taken me years. I wrote to Martin Buber and asked him for a short preface to the book. Buber was at the height of his popularity, and his name on the title page would have been particularly important. I waited a long time, and then a letter came from Buber. He assured me that he regarded Leo Baeck with respect and love. Baeck's teaching and person were extraordinarily important to him. But relations between him and Baeck were so complicated that he would have had to write a lengthy introduction rather than a short preface to the text, and unfortunately he did not have time for that. He regretted being unable to help.

The letter was longer than the preface I had hoped for. I

1

brooded on this and drafted a lengthy answer. In my second letter I reminded Buber of Franz Rosenzweig's last words from his mattress tomb: 'What does the Lodge think about Baeck's Mussolini decree?' Baeck had 'ordered' the B'nai B'rith order to buy a copy of the Buber-Rosenzweig translation of the Pentateuch for each of its members – around 12,000! A preface by Martin Buber for Baeck's last book, written in Terezin, could have had a similar effect. Was this not in a sense a debt of honour?

The letter to Buber lay on my desk for a week and then I tore it up. How could I dare to reproach the grand master of German Judaism in this way? It was *chutzpah* – brashness. Nevertheless, I still regret not having sent the letter. Perhaps a real encounter, some instruction, could have taken place. Instead of that, for decades I carried the letter I had torn up, the accusation, around with me in my bones. Because I did not achieve inner peace, an iron curtain grew up between me and the great teacher.

I once told this story to the poet Paul Celan. Remarkably, he had had a similar experience with Buber. With great hope and joy he had prepared for a meeting with Martin Buber by buying some of Buber's books, to have them signed by the great teacher. In a sense Paul Celan saw himself as one of the 'sages of Czernowitz'. Buber looked coldly at the books. 'They are the wrong editions,' he said, and refused to sign them. Celan felt completely shattered. The meeting was ruined, and he carried around with him this failure at dialogue, so that a wall grew up between him and the great teacher. Celan died too early to go on an inner journey to this fellow man. My journey came late, but it did come – unfortunately only after Buber's death. Inner conversion, *teshuva*, broke through the obstacles of my prejudices and made it possible for me to accept Buber's teachings.

What has this to do with my relationship to Germany and the Germans? The question brings us back to Rabbi Bunam. 'Seek peace in your place.' I am a man of peace, perhaps too peaceful and calm. '*Ohev shalom v'rodef shalom*', 'love peace and run after it,' say the sages. The love is there, but in my case perhaps the 'running' is more of a walk, though this also includes the road from Selma to Montgomery with Martin

Luther King. However, my inner career has not been as calm as might appear from outside. There are inhibitions, there is anxiety, there is rage and grief. To understand all this I had to embark on an inner journey which has its beginnings even before my experience on the so-called 'Kristallnacht'. Because I am a rabbi, this was ultimately a journey through the millennia (I am really 4000 years old!). The journey began in the present, like any journey. And my journal of what Dorothee Sölle calls 'the journey outward' goes via fellow men and women to God.

The sketches in this book derive from present-day experiences, above all from 1988, when for the first time since 1938 I spent a quite a long time in Germany. These are memories between two Kirchentage, of a semester as visiting professor at the Kirchliche Hochschule in Wuppertal. And here we come to the heart of my reflections. My relationship to Germany is based on a childhood of persecution. I left Germany in 1939 and I was never in a camp. In comparison to others, I have suffered little. But the Holocaust became the central theme of my research and my books, and my suffering as a child and my travelling in exile shaped my inner life. Here, within myself, lay the problem, and it was a long time before I returned to Germany. English became and now is my first language, and I had to learn again to address my fellow men and women and myself in German. As rabbi of an English congregation and as a teacher of future rabbis I had investigated myself, and this had brought me peace in certain areas. Now an iron curtain had to be broken. After fifty years I was again a Jew in Germany. And I had to find inner peace in order to be able to address my fellow men and women in peace.

The way that I found had been taken earlier by my teacher Leo Baeck. In 1952 he travelled the way through himself to the German people. The journal of this journey is in his work *Israel and the German People*. Here are the first sentences:

> Only someone moved by a deep, one might almost say a loving, desire for inner openness and outward clarity may speak about a peace between Israel and the German people. Only this truthfulness, in which thinking and speaking on a particular matter become one, so that there is no room for

3

afterthoughts and evasions, provides justification here for affirming or denying, hoping or despairing...

But now the other presupposition. It is as it were the *kairos* presupposition, with the question that it has to raise: supposing that this basis of the factual and the personal... is already there, will this controversy over peace also already begin now? Has the time for it come? There is an old Jewish saying: the one on whom the hour presses flees from it.

Has the time come? Some say... that the Jews should make their peace with time, with the joys and the sorrows of the time. With the joys, certainly, but also with the sorrows? Sorrow will unite with sorrow. But was there not something quite different still, and something quite different above all, in this time? Is peace to be concluded with all, with all the ways in which the image of God was to be destroyed?

Baeck's real question here was that of the 'reality of the German people today', after the slow healing of self-inflicted wounds. Is that dark period over? Time, says Kierkegaard, cannot be reversed, but it becomes past. Days follow days, years follow years. What do the children of time inherit from the past? How much of the demonic travelled through the shift in ages into the present? Should peace be concluded with evil?

The question takes different forms for Germans and for Jews, but it is the same question. It is the question of the journey outward to oneself. Each return creates something new. And, as Baeck says, 'Every true encounter stems from self-knowledge and creates new self-knowledge.' There were true encounters between me and Germany, between me and Germans. In the midst of the pine forest, in conversation with Heinrich von Trott zu Solz, I encountered the man and the people. The friendly living room in the house of Landesvater Johannes Rau in Wuppertal was an open door into a German world which bravely fought against sin. A small village community argued vigorously with me about the interpretation of New Testament texts relating to the death of Jesus; and my daily encounter with the students and teachers of the Kirchliche Hochschule in Wuppertal changed me inwardly.

Nothing was easy. My congregation in London had given

me leave for study and further education. Nevertheless, some of them were hurt when I changed my plans and wanted to spend my study time in Germany rather than Jerusalem. For many Jews Germany is and remains something impossible to cope with, a dark world not yet to be entered. Usually this is an attitude which recognizes the fact of a new Germany, but which cannot overcome the inner grief, the fear and consternation. That the rabbi wanted to spent his study time in this country, of all places, made a number of members of the congregation anxious. 'Jerusalem is so beautiful,' these friends told me. Quite! Jerusalem would have been sheer delight, a good rest and a feeling of redemption for me. I longed for that. I could have met friends every day. I would have found peace. But the grief in my bones, the dark nights of persecution, the incompleteness of my identity as a Jew and a child in Germany, would not have been answered. I wanted to go to Germany to find the beginning of an inner journey towards reconciliation. Reconciliation itself lies in the future, because I cannot determine the inner course of the Germans and Germany.

In my encounter with the other I can affirm my own identity and allow myself to be led to deeper self-knowledge, if there is a real encounter; but the other person must make the inner journey for him- or herself. In this book I may not speak for the others, and so I have little to say about German self-understanding. I shall be speaking of my experiences, my own development, my grief, my anxiety, my hopes. It is an attempt to describe the beginning of a journey towards reconciliation. The rest – more about the beginning, much more about the goal – is a work for the future.

And there is something else. I have always found it impossible to take myself seriously. A great danger for rabbis is that others take us too seriously. The term 'rabbi' prompts respect, and the individual gets caught up in this respect. This reverence, no, this divinization, destroyed Hasidism. The rabbis began to believe the legends about themselves. Only humour could save them. Here is a story.

Reb Azriel, the 'iron head', visited the seer of Lublin. 'I don't understand it,' he said. 'I am wiser than you, have greater knowledge, am more learned – but they all come to you, not to me. Why?' 'I don't understand it, either,' replied the holy seer. 'But perhaps this is the answer: you don't understand why the people don't come to you, and so they don't come to you. I don't understand why they come to me, and so they come to me.'

That was a sharp joke, an ironical reprimand. And I do not even have the problem of everyone coming to me. But I know that a rabbi stands on a stage (the word *bima*, pulpit, also means stage), as a model for the community. One always gives oneself, and the only sermon is one's own life. The tragic thing here is that only a few of us are so mature in our self-understanding that we can pass on a complete and authentic message. The members of the congregation make a model for themselves which for the most part exists only in their imaginations. Only a detail of this picture is really before them. So almost every rabbi I know has feelings of guilt, has now and then to get away from the congregation, lives in remorse and solitude. My students at Leo Baeck College, London, preparing for the rabbinate, also come to me and complain how difficult it is to take the first step into the world of the rabbis; how much they are suffering already – they can hardly go on studying. But Israel of Rizin, when asked by a sufferer unable to pray and learn because of his pain, replied: 'How do you know, friend, which is more pleasing to God, your teaching or your suffering?'

This question is put to everyone, and is a warning that ministers, teachers, pastors, should not take themselves too seriously, that we are not more exalted nor more holy than others who meet us. And so I am now writing about my encounters with fellow men and women, with the land of my youth and with the anxieties of my childhood.

Do not take it too seriously.

We also serve God in laughter.

A Preliminary Comment on the First Chapter

Most of the meetings described in this book took place in 1988. But history and life cannot be divided into tidy periods. Like Nelly Sachs' Samson I am falling through time, and so the first encounter with my Germany and my Germans that I am describing is one from 1984, the first step in my inner journey. Here I began to build the bridges which perhaps made later developments possible.

And à propos bridges, I shall also be describing my visits to the German Democratic Republic and want to begin by quoting a text connected with that. On 8 May 1985 there was a great Service of Remembrance in the Sophienkirche in East Berlin. Canon Paul Oestreicher and I were present as representatives of the Church of England. Paul read the greeting from Archbishop Robert Runcie, which said, among other things: 'I greet all the Christians who will be gathering in the German Democratic Republic in the presence of God on 8 May to commemorate the fortieth anniversary of the ending of the Second World War... I am very glad that you have a British delegation among them which includes a representative of the Jewish faith. By this sign the people of God bears witness that there is "neither Jew nor Greek, neither slave nor free, neither man nor woman". By this sign the church is building bridges which express more than our mutual penitence for the individual and collective sins of the past. By this sign we at the same time proclaim hope for reconciliation...'

In one sense the archbishop obliged me to take the work of reconciliation upon myself. I also lit one of the peace candles, stood in the group and went one step further towards reconciliation. A year previously, on 20 July 1984, there had been another event, more political than religious, but the religious dimensions emerged later in my life. It all fits together in the mosaic of my life – but that is quite natural in the life of a Jew.

Helmut Kohl, the
'Dispensation of Late Birth'
and Two Bodyguards

Really, the two bodyguards don't belong in this story at all, so we sent them off immediately. Evelyn, my wife, and I landed in Berlin and were received by the pair of them. 'Why this honour?', I asked – I had expected more. 'Look, Herr Rabbiner,' said one of them, 'when you give a lecture about the bomb plot on the 20th of July you arouse a certain amount of interest – perhaps in the wrong quarters.'

Evelyn and I looked at each other. She wanted to go straight to the KDW (the Harrods of Berlin) – should she take the policemen with her? Finally we agreed that we should keep this escort of honour as far as the hotel, and there we said good-bye to them. The whole thing was already difficult enough as it was. After forty years the events of the 20th of July – the attempt to blow up Hitler with a bomb – were for the first time to be recognized by an act of state. Chancellor Helmut Kohl had declared his readiness to make a speech, and President von Weizsäcker would also take part. The research group into the events of the 20th of July and the descendants of the resistance were at odds. For some people the whole thing was threatening to become too political, so the idea arose of giving the speech proper on the evening of the 19th and allowing the prominent politicians to say a few words at the wreath-laying the next day. But who was to give the speech?

A small group travelled to Arnoldshain, where Evelyn and I were attending a conference in the Martin Niemöller House of the Evangelical Academy. Eberhard Bethge and Rüdiger von Voss were the spokesmen. Because they could hardly turn down the Chancellor's offer, they especially wanted to have a serious scholarly and religious address about the 20th of July. Eberhard had suggested me as the speaker. Would I accept?

I hesitated.

'You know,' I said, 'if I gave such a lecture I would have to mention that this group of officers was only a minute part of the resistance against Hitler.' 'You are completely free to say whatever you want,' I was assured. 'In that case I would also have to mention that the real resistance after 1933 mostly came from Communists, and that the resistance in the ghetto and the camps is still underestimated.' 'There are no difficulties about that.'

I said yes, but with inner doubts and anxieties.

And now we were in Berlin, the city in which I was born. My last memory of the city was 'Kristallnacht', or rather, the pogrom night of 1938. I could still vividly remember the whole of that night. After that came the years of travel, and ultimately brief visits. These were not so much to the city as to friends of dialogue, above all Winfried Maechler and his Evangelical Academy, where we met – by the Wannsee! – as Jews, Christians and Muslims. For me these visits were quite separate from my childhood and youth. I once stood on the corner of Motzstrasse and Nollendorfplatz, where I had lived: now it is a parking lot. The Theodor Herzl school in Reichskanzlerplatz (Adolf-Hitler-Platz) was burnt down during my childhood. What was left? In fact, Berlin, a city with great character, with an individuality which attracted me, but to which I had not yet responded. Only once, with my PhD supervisor Jakob Taubes and with Rudi Dutschke... but that's another story.

Berlin, on the fortieth anniversary of the 20th of July. There were problems from the beginning. As Eberhard had told me, opposition to my visit had developed among the group of descendants of the resistance. Why had a *rabbi* to be invited, of all people? The Kreisau Circle – for all its good qualities – had never really been friendly to the Jews. Had the attempt on Hitler's life succeeded, Goerdeler would immediately have opened the concentration camps and put an end to the killing. But whether he would also immediately have repealed the anti-Jewish laws is a question to which there really isn't any answer. The struggle for the Jews and Judaism developed slowly in the life and writings of Dietrich Bonhoeffer, more slowly than in the Moltke family. But there were circles in this resistance group which then as now have to be described as reactionary. A contemporary comment today which Stuttgart's Mayor Rommel made to Mayor Teddy Kollek, 'Better lose with Hitler than win without Hitler', would not have met with approval in the 20th of July circles. The antiquated nationalism in this aristocratic group was quite dominant. So I had taken great trouble over my lecture, since I was also coming as a pastor to a memorial service and had to honour the parents of these descendants. Were they anxious about what I would say? At all events, the preparation had changed considerably because of this opposition. There was originally to have been a television transmission – now this was cancelled. The radio was there, and that was almost a surprise. No invitations had been sent to well-known personalities, and hardly any to the press. So it was almost a miracle that journalists were there at all. In short, the whole thing was to be transformed into a kind of private ceremony, so that my perhaps provocative speech would not be too disruptive.

The members of the research group itself were friendly, and in their meetings with us their behaviour was very correct. For many it was the first time they had met a rabbi, and some had never known a Jew. Evelyn was at first utterly dazed by her dealings with this nobility. Never had her hand been kissed so often. And then someone came up and introduced himself: 'Prince...' She waited expectantly: what nobleman would she meet now? The man repeated, 'Prinz... Georg Prinz, journalist.' It was good to be on firm ground again.

My lecture lasted just an hour, because it had been prepared with the planned television programme in view. There was deep silence in the Otto-Braun-Saal within the new State Library in Berlin, and I think that everyone listened very attentively. In his introduction to the book which was later published by Neske Verlag, Rüdiger von Voss wrote:

Zachor V-shamor b'dibur echad: remember and keep memory alive. Just as all the other days are created for the sake of the one Sabbath day, so all other words are given us for the sake of the one word. Remember!

Albert H.Friedlander quoted these words of Elie Wiesel in the lecture which he gave on 19 July 1984 in the Otto-Braun-Saal in Berlin to the survivors and descendants of the German resistance. Albert H.Friedlander spoke on the one hand in his spiritual capacity as rabbi of the Westminster Synagogue, and on the other in his academic capacity as Director of the Leo Baeck College in London. For the first time in post-war Germany a citizen of this land who had become a victim of persecution by the National Socialist rule of violence had won through to return to his homeland on such a day to give a sign of remembrance and reconciliation.

With great earnestness Albert H.Friedlander pointed out that no one can say farewell to the past, to Auschwitz, as long as the 20th of July 1944 is rightly acknowledged. The ethical significance of this historical event is made clear by the dimensions of 'too late' and 'too little'. The dictatorship was not overthrown. Man triumphed, in that it was shown that the human can overcome the inhuman.

From the depths of his faith, Rabbi Friedlander warned against making martyrs of the men and women of the resistance and at the same time removing them so far from those alive today that their legacy can no longer have any effect. Reflection on resistance, Friedlander made clear, brings with it an obligation to resist evil every day, not to become accomplices of it again, where law and freedom are suppressed.

Rüdiger had rightly heard the 'too little' and 'too late'. And he had also heard my comment that there were moments in which humanity had triumphed over inhumanity – an admonition to the many who had thought such a venture impossible. I combined the mourning of this hour with Paul Celan's 'Straitening'; I had spoken of the covering up, the word, the ashes, the moist eyes. There had to be shared mourning for the past and also for the present. I wanted to speak to people, not just friends like Eberhard Bethge and

Dietrich Goldschmidt, but all those who were facing the past. In the words of Elie Wiesel, I said:

> I belong to a people whose suffering is as old as the suffering of the earth. I belong to a people which keeps memory alive. My people is a people of history... all other words are given to us for the sake of this one word: remember!

We thought of the resistance: in the ghettoes, in the camps, on the streets and also in the group of their parents, who had sacrificed their lives in this resistance. Was resistance against the state justified? They could also have learned this from the writings of Bonhoeffer. The men (and women) of the resistance were witnesses to the fact that resistance was possible, and that remains their great gift to their land and to their children. And I spoke about more recent historical efforts to rise above the 'collective guilt of the Germans' to a new stage of consciousness and responsibility which would not veil the historical truth. 'We must reflect on the events of the past to find the way to identity,' I said. Why was there not a fight against Hitler from the beginning? And I quoted Helmut Gollwitzer: 'Our culpable neglect did not lie in this time, but earlier... We should have spoken more openly.'

That this insight was also still valid today also found expression in my concluding words:

> The world must be newly saved every day. Every day we must resist evil; we must guard against becoming guilty of new catastrophes. And every day should become a day of recollection, a day of love and shared humanity. Every day.

Many people came up to me that evening and on the following day to express their gratitude and understanding. Not all, but far more than I had expected. And we took part in the public ceremony the next day at which Helmut Kohl, Richard von Weizsäcker, Eberhard Diepgen and Klaus von Dohnanyi spoke. Not everything in these speeches was appropriate. The Chancellor spoke with praise for the attack on the Hitler state – and by so doing wanted to demonstrate that nowadays such an attack on the democratic state would be unjust. Some historians had already attempted in the week before this day to look at history in the light of a 'new objectivity'. In my address I had warned that 'our own history must not drive out real history', which was what was being attempted at the time. 'We may never exclude Auschwitz and the reality of this structure,' I said. If we find the way to the heroic in this dark time, we must also be aware that evil is part of it, part of the same heritage. 'Problems are not resolved by a heroic myth,' I commented. At a time of mourning, when this group was thinking of their fathers with devotion, I could not draw them into a confession of guilt, nor did I want to – but I had to associate them in shared suffering with Jews, Sinti and Communists. I saw this as a first step.

People nowadays speak of the 'dispensation of late birth', and this means the attempt to get away from one's own history. But in that case this group would have had to abandon their parents, for the darkness and the brightness in the past are one. Helmut Schmidt's adviser, Günter Gaus, coined this saying about the 'dispensation of late birth', and interpreted it thus: it is a gift of grace that we can now take responsibility, that we can set to this work on the past because we were not born until after it. But Helmut Kohl's advisor is Herr Stürmer, the fighter in historical disputes, who wants to relativize this very responsibility, and who allowed Chancellor Kohl to dissociate himself from guilt, in Israel of all places. One can only speak of the 'dispensation of late birth' when at the same time one assumes responsiblity. But perhaps Herr Kohl has not yet said his last word on the matter. We sat together on the 20th of July. His first words to me were, 'Did you know that I have a doctorate in history?' I didn't...

We left Berlin the next day. However, I also want to say something in favour of Helmut Kohl. Evelyn did not sit next to me at the VIP table – the decision was called 'protocol' – but was placed elsewhere, which wasn't to my liking. So Eberhard Bethge took the Chancellor to Evelyn's table, and he spoke with her very cordially, and was most friendly. The evening was more enjoyable. We had a good round table with friends for our meal in the restaurant of the Hotel Berlin.

Was this the Berlin of my past? Not at all. Nowadays Berlin speaks to me mostly through books. And films. I read hundreds

13

of thrillers a year. For me Berlin remains the spy centre of the world: le Carré, Deighton. Berlin is the city of Harry Palmer. And suddenly he was sitting there. At the next table! Michael Caine and some friends were sitting at a nearby table, perhaps after television work in Berlin. I looked for my fountain pen.

'Control yourself,' muttered Evelyn gently. 'But.. Harry Palmer, I mean Michael Caine...' I stammered. 'Certainly not,' she said. And the film star was left in peace.

Günther Neske was at our table and asked for permission to print my address. He had been the first to publish the poems of Paul Celan and had liked the quotations – as had Heinrich von Trott zu Solz, who became a friend at this time because of Paul Celan. I saw Richard von Weizsäcker again, years later, in the Goethe Institute in London. I gave him two copies. 'Why?' he asked. 'I've dedicated one copy to you,' I said. 'Now please sign the second for me!' He laughed, and did me the honour. The book is called *Reconciliation with History*. We haven't got that far yet, but something has begun, not least in these personal meetings.

Only I wish I had got 'Harry Palmer's' autograph in Berlin.

Wuppertal

It is difficult to live with a saint. I always feel sorry for Evelyn, and have much sympathy with her. In Judaism, everyone is holy. But some of us wear a halo in public and suffer from headaches. The halo is neither an honour or a distinction. But rabbis, doctors, social workers, in short, all those who have found their place in the 'serving' professions, are regarded as public saints.

Yet one has to be mean. At last one sits down in the family circle, with the firm promise to devote this evening solely to the family. The telephone rings. At one time we simply took the receiver off the hook, but then the new technology won. After a minute the new telephone begins to roar, 'You have not replaced the receiver', and then it goes on shrilling until the receiver has been replaced. It rings yet again. I reply, and the family evening has gone by the board. A visit to the hospital? A member of the congregation has a problem which must be resolved immediately? A death in the congregation? The family always comes last, and firm promises are not kept: but the rabbi's reputation for holiness is burnished bright once again.

Recently the telephone rang at 3 a.m. A call from the hospital: 'You must come at once – a woman is dying.' I dressed, said good-bye to Evelyn, knowing that she would not get back to sleep again, and twenty minutes later was in the ward. Death had been quicker, but at least I could say the prayers for the dead, sit with the family and look after them and comfort them. After a while it became clear to me that this family was strictly Orthodox, and that as a 'progressive' rabbi I did not have their confidence. 'Why did you call me in particular?' I asked. 'Why

15

do you think?' came the furious retort. 'We couldn't have woken up our revered rabbi. He would never have forgiven us.'

I congratulated myself on the honour they had bestowed on me and mentioned that I had come in a taxi. Could they now order a taxi for my journey home? 'The nurse will be able to arrange that,' was the answer, and the family turned away from me to discuss the important questions. Who was not to be told of the death (the old family dispute!), what papers had to be informed? I left the group, found a taxi and happily returned home to wake Evelyn up again – she had gone back to sleep. But indignation at this story robbed her of sleep for the rest of the night. She had only one word for her saint: 'Idiot.' And she often has occasion to use this word.

The call to Wuppertal, to teach there for a semester on the 'holy mount', as a visiting professor at the Kirchliche Hochschule, freed me for a while from this system. For a long time I had been asking the congregation to grant me a 'sabbatical', a year's vacation after six years' service (which had already grown into sixteen, but who counts that accurately?). The congregation asked me to wait another year, and then was prepared to release me for five months. It was to be a time of study for me. But where? First of all I thought, like any rabbi, of Jerusalem. But would I study there? I know myself only too well. Jerusalem is my paradise on earth. Every day I would visit friends and enjoy this city, but I would not learn, and I would write very little. The invitation to Wuppertal would make this time something different for me. I had to face my problems; it would be hard work, but important. As a rabbi, as a Jewish teacher at a Christian college, I would rediscover the problems of my life in the problems of the students and teachers there. There could be, there had to be, an encounter. Only I was afraid that I might fail. And in my daily life I have so much support from Evelyn that the loneliness there oppressed me; could I and should I go into this loneliness?

My decision was based on my hope that this journey would also be a journey inwards. And that is what happened. Encounter and dialogue took place, and I learned a good deal in this teaching semester. I not only met people, but my surroundings, the area, the mountain spoke to me. We live in an extraordinary time: time and space remain a mystery for human beings, and become more mysterious the more one investigates them. Today's scientists create histories and legends which are meant to bring us to the origin of all things, but which only push the limits of understanding further into the distance. The investigation of matter, the infinitely small and the infinitely large, in quantum physics, or as an ingredient of a new cosmology, only confronts us with new mysteries. Electrons move in all possible directions and appear to be in two places at the same time. Scientific calculations put the sub-atomic particles at the place which had been hoped for. Legends and histories become true, the stars follow the structures devised for them and wait to be discovered by us. Kepler, Copernicus and Einstein have told us the stories which introduce us to the mysteries of the environment. New narrators, new scientists, will bring us new mysteries with the legends of our time. The word creates the world, like the cabbalistic interpretation of the history of creation described in the Zohar.

Such thoughts surrounded me when I landed in Wuppertal. The scientists seemed to be far removed from the 'holy mountain', from the Kirchliche Hochschule. But I found that the theological ideas, the stories and legends, were closely connected with the stories of the cosmologists. I say this not as an attack but in support. I did not come as a rabbi to enter into a polemical relationship with the Christian theologians of Wuppertal. My visit was not meant to be a confrontation between Judaism and Christianity. We met to discuss problems of religion together, and to share our experiences with one another. One of my seminars was on the theme of 'The Science of Judaism and Heinrich Heine'. I knew that the students liked studying Heine, but I was particularly keen to talk about 'The Science of Judaism', about the modern attempt to put the sphere of religion into science, with its rigorous thought, its logical laws and the researches of experts. The 'Association for the Culture and Science of the Jews', founded in 1819, brought together the great young thinkers of that time: Leopold Zunz, Eduard Gans, Heinrich Heine, Wohlwill, Jost, and many others, who wanted to create a place for themselves as Jews within Western culture. It was at that time the historians and not the physicists who dominated the thought and research of the century. Religion developed its own thinking, built on the discoveries of archaeology and the insights of philosophy, and already at this early period of modern thought learned that dreams and legends have their own place, and that one cannot simply quantify them and destroy them through logical analysis. The dialogue between religion and science at that time seemed to me to be important for today's situation.

I had many teachers in Wuppertal. Without wanting to insult my friends, I have to give pride of place to the Hochschule cat. He was a theologian. I met him every day, on the way to the library. He lay in the sun and avoided the advancing shadows with the certainty of a sleepwalker. His doctrine was simple: one has to find the sun, and one has to stay in the sun. Darkness is rejected, and light is seized with both paws.

My second teacher was the 'holy mountain' itself. The landscape was part of it: the views, the Bismarck Tower nearby, and the famous suspended railway in the distance. I found the narrow path which led downwards; in seven minutes I could get to the shops, buy things at the grocery store, visit the bakery. But the way back took twenty five minutes or more, depending how much one had bought. John Bunyan's *Pilgrim's Progress* leads through the Slough of Despond and ascends to the Delectable Mountains. The environment reflects our inner world. My disquiet and loneliness, my longings and my dreams, were alive in the landscape. In the weeks and months that I spent in Wuppertal they changed, because they had to bow to other laws of the environment. An almost hallowed rest can be found on this mountain. I lived in the Hochschule, and the past and present of a particular Christian history of faith clung to more than the people whom I encountered. The rainy mountain itself had its own secrets. One has to climb the mountain in the cloud, the rain, and the darkness of twilight: it was always a stage of the inner journey.

The students gave me many opportunities for development, dialogue, and also disappointment. We first met in the refectory. I changed my table regularly, in order to get to know new students. It could be very disappointing – one could sit at the table and remain invisible, although the students were always very polite. A conversation usually developed when students from my seminar sat at the table. I listened a lot and said little. Behind the jokes and chatter I could often detect a great deal of uncertainty, almost despair: the church was presenting the beginners with great problems, including economic ones. But occasionally we had theological discussions which we could never bring to an end. One wall in the dining room has an enlargement of a photograph on it: the march from Montgomery with Martin Luther King. I looked at the wall to try to find myself in it (in the third row), but unfortunately in this photograph I was obscured by someone else. But the word got around that I had taken part in the march, and that prompted some conversations in the refectory.

A sabbath meal with students was a real encounter. Evelyn and our daughter Ariel visited me on the way back from a trip to Prague. Both were tired after a long car journey and were looking forward to a good meal with me at the best restaurant in town. 'Impossible,' I said with regret, 'I've invited twenty students to a sabbath meal in my room. You've arrived just in time to help me with it.'

Soon the students appeared in my room, bringing vegetarian food, crockery, cutlery (I thought I had seen some of it in the refectory) and tables and chairs borrowed from neighbours. Without Evelyn and Ariel it would not have been a proper sabbath celebration: the prayers for candles and wine, the grace after meals and then the Z'mirot (sabbath songs) were possible only because the two of them were present – I am banned from singing in my family. It was a lively, friendly evening, with many questions and answers. In this atmosphere I could really speak about Judaism and explain the rabbinic interpretations of the biblical texts in a way which matched the experience of this evening, and could show the students the special significance of the Jewish tradition. The table again became an altar and the table fellowship a community which could meet in shared biblical traditions. However, we had to be careful not to misuse this experience; the recognition of Judaism within Christianity, the encounter with Jewish customs within the life of Jesus, are sometimes abused, in that Judaism is simply regarded as a preparation for Christianity. For that very reason, it was so important that this evening should not be an academic study of the sabbath. The students took part in the Friedlander family's celebration of the sabbath, shared in our joy, and recognized that there is an authentic religious life quite independently of Christianity and outside it. But a boundary was crossed, and after this evening I was much closer to the students. When Evelyn and Ariel went away again two days later it was more lonely than before, although there was a new, deeper bond with the students.

'Look for a teacher and find a fellow student,' teaches the Talmud (Pirke Avot). I found both on the holy mountain.

The Ephorus of the Hochschule, Siegward Kunath, was able to introduce me to the mountain because he had a special relationship to my own mountain. In his book of poems about Israel (*Im Lande: Impressionen aus Israel*), he brought me his poem:

Temple Mount

> Curves, stairways, stone walls –
> between the mosques
> the fountains,
> for the Messiah
> the closed door.
>
> So the square
> of wall and sun
> covers the mountain
> to which Abraham raised his eyes,
> ready to sacrifice his son.
>
> His altar
> of rough-hewn rock
> has long been secured
> under the cupola,
> in the twilight
> of magical colours.
>
> Sacrifices die
> elsewhere.

Three world religions meet on this mountain, and the present recognizes itself again as a moment between the past and the future. Siegward knows this in his unique way, and in our meeting on 'his' mountain we found a special insight between us into our mutual traditions. Another quite special bridge between us was Heinrich Heine. The seminar on Heine and the Science of Judaism was a joint one in which Siegward did most of the teaching. As a member of the Heine-Gesellschaft he also guided our group through the Heine Museum in Düsseldorf, and I looked at the poet's letters and writings, especially the letters to his mother, with a feeling of close affinity. Heine's career as a Jew and a German remains disputed. His baptism is usually completely misunderstood, and it is forgotten that he only undertook this step to get an 'entry ticket', as 'stealing silver spoons was not allowed'.

Heine wanted to attain the supreme goal in the cultural and political life of the Germany of his time: he wanted to become a professor. Nowadays people no longer understood how lofty a creature a professor was in his day. The professor was a god, high on Olympus. But to become professor of history at a German university, appointed by the state, one had to become a full citizen of the state, i.e. Christian and German. Jews were outside the system. In the last resort, could a Jew really teach Christian theology or the history of the state and church? Heine did not want to be baptized. Our fascinating discussion on the 'Association for Jewish Culture and Science' therefore centred on the problem of how a Jew can remain a Jew and nevertheless play a full part in this culture.

Eduard Gans, Hegel's amanuensis and successor at Berlin University, hoped that the Association would provide a solution. Jews were not to teach Christianity, but the new science now saw the different spheres of religion in a new way. It was recognized that Judaism, too, was now to undergo a rigorous investigation by science. Judaism thus became a new discipline within university study. Here Jews could be and had to be appointed to teach this new discipline. Here new chairs could be created, for Jews. In America this idea has become established only in the last twenty years – it was too early for Germany at the beginning of the nineteenth century. The plan collapsed, and the Association with it. Many of its members, Gans, Heine, Lehmann, went over to Christianity. Gans became Hegel's successor, and Heine became – Heine. But the problems were not solved. They remained accusations and grief for our time. We could not cover all the dimensions in our seminar, although we also contrasted 'Junges Deutschland' to some extent with the 'young Palestine group'. Ludwig Börne – the Löb Baruch from the Judengasse in Frankfurt – visited our group. The dispute between Heine and Börne, the shared 'Jewish grief', the 'Letters from Paris', and so much else, became a shared labour of love for Siegward and me, which was also recognized by the students. And when we also brought in Rachel Varnhagen von Ense and the Berlin salons, the cup overflowed. We could only concede that we had introduced the problems into the thought-world of the students and express the hope that this would lead to further thought and also work on their part.

Once, when the young Heine was obeying a summons to the police station in Berlin, he was asked, 'And what are your political views, Herr Heine?' He replied, 'Just like those of the government – none at all.'

As a result he became a marked man. They knew what he was: an outsider, a mocker who dared to criticize the government. A Jew! That is why I had chosen this theme. We were not just talking about Heine. We were also talking about me, about the Jew who has a close relationship to German culture, to the German state, to the land. It makes hardly any difference whether one is ostracized or recognized. Moses Mendelssohn critized Frederick the Great for speaking French instead of devoting himself to German. And he also dared to publish a sharp judgment on Frederick's poems: 'If the king writes as a poet he must be treated as a poet.' The criticism comes inside and outside culture. But if one accepts the criticism, then the dimensions of one's own life grow. This was my hope for the work in Wuppertal. And the criticism of the students and the admonitions of Siegward came at the same time and instructed me.

Wuppertal also meant new friendships, which instructed me in new ways. First of all I found it remarkable that the small boy in my house was called Sören – but his father was a Kierkegaard scholar. In long evening conversations between Uwe Seelbach, his wife Pia, and myself, I arrived at new ideas, particularly about the way of dialogue which had been prompted by these friends. A warm, good friendship arose and still exists, which developed at a time when I was often lonely. I again learned that a glass of wine and a chat is important.

My greatest debt of gratitude for instruction and ongoing friendship I owe to Bertold Klappert, with whom I collaborated day and night. We were also bound together by a common love: we shared Leo Baeck as a great teacher. And so every Wednesday evening we had a gathering which studied his late work. The text was *This People: Jewish Existence*, written in the concentration camp. But the book had to be seen through Baeck's life, and so we used the first pages of my Baeck biography, which have appeared in a book about the saints of world religion.

'Patchwork,' said the seer of Lublin to his pupil, who was stumbling to and fro between the obstacles and disturbances on the way of asceticism. Martin Buber reflected a good deal on this remark. Had the young Hasid not done his best, was he not ready to sacrifice his pride? Why was there blame now, instead of praise? Later Buber understood Jaakob Jizchak's teaching. The seer was warning against any attempt which would not lead to a higher level. The to-ing and fro-ing, the zig-zag character of action, is suspicious: what is wanted is work that is all of a piece, not 'patchwork'. The sage of Lublin wanted to teach that a man may unite his soul.

> The man with a manifold, complicated, contradictory soul is not delivered: the innermost part of this soul, the power of God in its depths, may have an effect on it, may unite it…
>
> What the seer criticized the Hasid for was that he had undertaken his venture with a soul which was not made one: the union cannot come about in the midst of the work (Martin Buber).

Of course Buber knew that the soul can never finally be made one. The great 'saints' struggle for unity, lapse again, but also note that the way leads to a more constant unity – albeit by detours in which the whole person finds himself (i.e., according to Martin Buber, body and soul together – 'the person who in this way becomes a unity of body and spirit, whose work is of a piece').

Leo Baeck was such a person: leader of the German Jews in the hardest of times, teacher in Terezin, to whom Selma Stern-Täubler rightly accorded the title of the Josel of Rosheim: 'Commander of Jewry in the Holy Roman Empire of the German Nation'. Here was 'work all of a piece'; here teaching and life in a tragic period were a testimony to the power of God in the depths of the soul. Baeck was not a Hasid – that is not a title to be applied to a cool, enlightened, Western intellectual, though his teaching is a good supplement to Hasidism. He was not a prophet like Jeremiah. He was the centre of Jewish organizations, the *primus inter pares*, a political figure, although ultimately he must be seen as the great rabbi, whose work and teaching in the darkest of times turned away from the centre of politics, or power, precisely because he recognized the degree to which this power can be abused. But like Jaakob Jizchak and also like Jeremiah, his person can express doubts: has he taken on too much? Is he stumbling? Were there wrong decisions at a difficult time?

We are talking of a person and not of a legend. The answer to all this must be yes: he made mistakes, he made the wrong decisions, just as every historian can accuse the protagonists of the past of the same thing. Our 'saints' remain human beings, imperfect, with mistakes and weaknesses and inconsistencies. 'Noah was a righteous man in his generation,' says the Bible. And the interpreters of scripture argue as to whether this amounts to a relativization. Does it mean that in a time of evil people, the ordinary person is an extraordinary righteous figure? Finally they came to say that if Noah remained steadfast at a time in which evil triumphed, he was really a perfect righteous man – for any time. We must say the same thing here: Baeck was a righteous man, a great man, who faced circumstances and proved himself.

We must even look at legends critically – and that has often been done. But behind the legend there is a man, a rabbi, a great soul. The Hasidic Rebbes had their pupils, their disciples. The great Western teachers of Judaism also had their disciples. Baeck, Buber, Rosenzweig and others have – or would have had – followers; but in the twentieth century, in the time of Auschwitz, they all disappeared. In Germany there was only one master – death. What remained was the teaching, but also the life, a model for our time. A subjective element also enters into this account of a 'saint in Judaism': Leo Baeck was my teacher. And just as the Hasidim imitated and followed their teachers in all things, in the lacing of their boots and the way they wore their coats as much as the interpretation of the text, so I can clearly remember long walks through forest and snow, walks without words, or listening to a conversation between Baeck and other teachers, whispering and silence – all this plays a part in this story, is the concluding word to a teaching which can be found in the most important Jewish books of our time.

The following extract from my biography of Leo Baeck may perhaps be an introduction to this life; it takes on special importance in the search for the character of holiness in people.

Far too much refuse had been placed in the garbage wagon. It moved through the grey rain of the camp with infinite slowness, a hateful, heavy thing, chaining its 'beasts of burden' to the filth from which there was no escape. Its miasma clogged their pores. Its weight cut into shoulders, arms and legs as foot was carefully placed before trembling foot and the cart was inched on its way past the barracks. Every once in a while the cart came to a halt, to load, to unload. Filthy, tired, trembling from their exertions in the harsh winter atmosphere, the beasts of burden turned towards one another:

'But my dear Professor,' said one to the other, 'surely you would not ignore the actions of the protagonists in the *Symposium*? Even the directions in which the glasses move have significance. And the stormy entrance of Alcibiades – your students at Leiden must have connected this with the text? Or do you think...'

'I'm sorry, Dr Baeck,' interrupted the other beast of burden, 'but the guard is motioning us on. Wait until we've turned the corner.' And the garbage cart continued on its way through the streets of Terezin, Hitler's 'model' concentration camp, which he had 'given' to the Jews.

The next week, Leo Baeck would be seventy years old. A tall, imposing, bearded figure, he had been judged strong enough to be one of the beasts of burden for the camp. Behind that judgment there lurked the insidious hope that the work would break and destroy this man. Terezin did not gas its victims. Starvation, hardships, exposure to the elements and fever were enough to destroy its prisoners by the thousand. For those who survived, there were periodic transports and 'resettlement' in the East. But there were special circumstances for Leo Baeck. The quicker his spirit was broken, his dignity besmirched, his moral and physical strength shattered, the more certain would be the approval from Berlin and from Eichmann himself. For Leo Baeck, after all, was not just any Jew taken by the Nazis and thrown into the blazing furnace of Hitler's 'Final Solution'; he was the leader of German Jewry, the last duly elected and appointed leader of a community which had come to an end after more than a thousand years of historic existence. He was one of the great scholars of his generation; what he had to say about Christianity, mysticism or ancient philosophy was received with as much attention as his great writings on the essence of Judaism. Grandmaster of the German B'nai B'rith fraternal organization of Jews, the leading rabbi of the Jewish community of Berlin, professor of the last Jewish seminary in Germany still secretly ordaining young men as rabbis to a dying community, Leo Baeck had refused to leave Germany – despite the insistence of Jews all over the world, of the German leaders themselves. Now, after five arrests and much suffering, he had come to Terezin.

The days and nights of Terezin – Theresienstadt, the Germans called it – have been described by others who survived. Reports of it had already come back to Leo Baeck. Three of his sisters had died there; a fourth one died shortly after he arrived. And now he was there himself, one of the many so-called important prisoners who had once been considered the great men of the age by the surrounding world. Here, they were to be mocked, to be broken, to be used as puppets in the ghastly games of the Nazis. For there were times when the outside world was to be permitted a glimpse of the camp. The sick and dying were crammed into the upper stories of the barrracks – visiting dignitaries cannot be bothered to climb a staircase – musicians were forced to play, clean blankets were issued for the day, and those who really did not want to know the truth could fool themselves into the belief that things were not really so bad, after all.

Baeck did not permit himself and them to be used. He took his place in the camp as no.187894, beast of burden for the refuse cart or any other tasks the warders assigned to him. But they could not stop a beast of burden discussing philosophy with its neighbour; and they could not stop him from being himself, a rabbi, a teacher.

Metals are heated in the furnace to the point where all foreign matter is melted away, where only the essence remains. In the fiery hell of the concentration camp Baeck's essence revealed itself: he was a rabbi. He would not take an active role in the internal administration of the camp, even as a member of the Council of Elders. There was power there, power which could corrupt – extra days of life beckoned to those in authority. Certainly someone had to serve in those councils; but many were available for that task. Other tasks presented themselves to Baeck in those days and nights of Terezin. The sick had to be comforted; the dying had to be seen to; death needed the dignity of ritual. And the living had to be taught. Terezin needed its teacher.

The beast of burden was able to turn to other tasks, to teaching and to preaching. Baeck was available to all inmates of the camp. It is often forgotten how many Christians found their way into this hell – one Jewish grandparent was enough to qualify someone for admittance. These people lived in a particular anguish of their own. Often strong in their Christian faith, they had no religious instruction and worship here; they lacked the consolations of their faith at a moment when these were desperately needed. They learned to come to Leo Baeck, to be instructed and comforted by him. They, too, called him rabbi.

And out of Terezin there came the word of Torah.

What did the inmates learn? And were there seeds which survived the flames and left a harvest for the days which followed, for our own times?

Wild beasts in uniform roamed the streets of Terezin, guarded its gates, and tried to stamp out the humanity still flickering in the thin grey faces of the prisoners. They could not succeed, for late at night, crowded together tightly in a small barrack room which could not contain them all, the prisoners sacrificed vital hours of rest in order to listen to Leo Baeck and to others, who lectured to them on Plato, Aristotle, on Greek and Roman philosophy. Using his fantastic memory, Baeck quoted page after page of the writings of the great historians Thucydides and Herodotus. Darkness covered the camp, the room. Only his voice was heard, weak, melodic, low but very clear, evoking other times and places. In the crowded little room, the prisoners were aware that the very act of listening amounted to a rebellion, an uprising against the inhumanity of their captors, an assertion of their own humanity. And so they listened to Leo Baeck; not because he was a scholar enabling them to pose as civilized people, but because he was their rabbi, who taught them that their humanity need not be extinguished.

The garbage wagon rolled on through the mud and snow of the alley. It turned the corner. Somewhere in the distance, an incongruous sound hung in the heavy air – the musicians of Terezin were rehearsing Verdi's *Requiem*. It was their final rehearsal: after the performance, they would be sent to Auschwitz in one transport. Nearby, in a barracks, a child drew a picture of a butterfly on a scrap of paper, looked around, and wrote a little poem underneath, 'But I have never seen a butterfly here'. Two streets away, a tired prisoner slumped to the ground and moved no more. And, around the corner, the two beasts of burden stopped again, and turned once more to one another: 'The clearest definition of love in Plato's sense may be found in the myth which is told as the climax of the *Symposium.*'

In the darkness of Terezin, men continued to feel themselves fashioned in God's image, reaching towards the light.

We too reach towards the light, but there must be people to show the way. In moments of his life Baeck was perhaps a saint, although I cannot recognize this word in Judaism. But at every moment and in every word Baeck was a teacher, and so we met in our study in Wuppertal.

Wuppertal and Leo Baeck

Why did these Protestant students want to hear so much about Leo Baeck? Partly, of course, because they had no choice. Bertold Klappert and I had made the decision about my lectures and seminars from the beginning, and Bertold was convinced that this topic was the most important for the students to study. At the end of the semester the students agreed. Leo Baeck was a name that they had already heard, a representative of German Judaism. They did not know more, except perhaps that some of his books on Judaism and also on the New Testament were on the library shelves.

The library. Shortly before my arrival a large room had been cleared and marked out for Judaica. It was a very good choice, but the shelves were still quite empty. 'Don't you have any Jewish encyclopaedias?', I asked in some perplexity. 'Oh, those are in the Old Testament room,' I was told. Next day they were in the Judaica room. But people were confused when they heard my next question, above all because I termed it 'my last territorial demand': 'Give me the whole of the "Old Testament" – my Hebrew Bible!'

I myself knew that this enormous collection would never fit in my small room, but I wanted my colleagues to think about it and to draw the boundaries of Jewish tradition rather wider.

In my first series of lectures I attempted to understand the study of Judaism at the Kirchliche Hochschule since 1980. The responsibility for this teaching arose out of a decision of the Rhineland Synod to create a correct and penitent relationship between Judaism and Christianity. Every two years a Jewish visiting professor was to visit the Hochschule for a semester and offer one or two events there.

So at the beginning of the first series of lectures I mentioned my predecessors, whose work had already contributed a good deal to this Christian-Jewish dialogue. The first was Pinchas Lapide, a brilliant speaker, exegete and apologist for Judaism. His dialogues with the great theologians in Germany are famous, and his work at the Hochschule certainly brought new young partners into Christian-Jewish dialogue. The next was Michael Wyschogrod, a profound Orthodox theologian from New York, extremely learned. He was and is a great man. My immediate predecessor was Rabbi Wolfgang Hamburger, a splendid example of a human rabbi. Wolfgang studied with me in Cincinnati and brought authentic Jewish life and religion to the students.

Now I was in the series: rabbi of a well-known London congregation, first Director and now Dean of Leo Baeck College for training Reform rabbis, and also the biographer of Leo Baeck. What could I offer the students? Bertold Klappert suggested that I should give a systematic description of Baeck's theological development in the 1920s. These years are of decisive importance in Christianity: Barth, Brunner, Tillich, Gogarten – there were so many teachers at that time, and dialectical theology had a great influence. And at that time Baeck also was writing important works and developing his 'religion of polarity' in connection with the thought of Hermann Cohen, Franz Rosenzweig and Martin Buber. But more than this, Baeck stood in the Jewish world as a rabbi, teacher and president of institutions which guided public Jewish life. The 1920s were a special time in German culture. Jewish influence was by no means small. What, I asked the students, if I were to discuss not the theology but the cabaret of this time: Kurt Weill, Claire Waldorf? Have you read Kurt Pinthus? Have you studied Max Liebermann and the Berlin Secession? Shouldn't we visit the Roman Cafe with Kurt Tucholsky, Egon Kisch and Oskar Homolka? Believe me, I told the students, Leo Baeck will be more interesting than all that. The most stimulating area of the 1920s remains theology. Baeck's 'romantic religion' and his interpretations of the Midrash are more exciting and more important for our time of desolation and loneliness.

Midrash? What is that? The rabbinic interpretation of holy

scripture, a kind of preaching, of homiletic. And to introduce students to the thought-world of Leo Baeck in a roundabout way, I gave my own sermon, my midrashic thought, on a biblical text (Genesis 37.17ff.). I read and translated the Hebrew text – not because I though many people knew Hebrew, but to remind them of the sound of the words, the language, and the development of Hebrew thought.

Joseph was ordered by his father to find his brothers.

> And a man found him wandering in the fields; and the man asked him, 'What are you seeking?' 'I am seeking my brothers,' he said, 'Tell me, I pray you, where they are pasturing the flock.'

et achai ani m'vakesh: I am seeking my brothers. The good Pope John used this biblical passage when he was visiting a Jewish group. It is an invitation to dialogue. But midrash requires more of us. The collection of the Midrash Rabba always begins with a biblical saying which apparently has nothing to do with the theme and the text. It is just a gate through which we enter the biblical thought-world.

The 'unknown person in the fields' – this theme alone could occupy someone for years – shows Joseph the way. And where does this way lead?

> So Joseph went after his brothers, and found them at Dothan. They saw him afar off, and before he came near to them they conspired against him to kill him. They said to one another, 'Here comes this dreamer. come now, let us kill him and throw him into one of the cisterns; then we shall say that a wild beast has devoured him, and we shall see what will become of his dreams.'

We know the story. But what would this text sound like if we translated it into the language of the twentieth century? *achad ha-borot*, 'one of the cisterns'. Why not 'some dark valley called Babi Yar'? Why not 'a gas oven'? That is how people dealt with one another, even yesterday.

'Here comes the *baal hachalamot*, the master of dreams.' Who were the masters of the dreams of our time? They were called Sigmund Freud and Albert Einstein and Franz Kafka. They were also called Leo Baeck and Viktor Frankl and Paul Celan and Elie Wiesel. In the attempt to approach Leo Baeck we must visit the darkest valleys of our landscape, and we must then find the way back. In study together, in the doctrines of Judaism, in encounter with the great teacher, we found the way back, to new brotherhood. That is also Joseph's story. The biblical story shows us the brother among the brothers, Judah, who saved Joseph. Joseph does not die, although he undertakes the journey into the underworld of the slaves and so experiences something of death. In the end, Joseph and the brothers again meet face to face:

> And he wept aloud... And Joseph said to his brothers, 'I am Joseph... Joseph whom you sold into Egypt. And now do not be distressed, for God sent me before you to preserve life... not you, but God...' And he kissed all his brothers and wept upon them; and after that his brothers talked with him...

Any story, any man and any people are unique. But our reflections on history and theology brought us to a comparative study of the Christian and the Jewish teacher. Leo Baeck's favourite teacher of history was Leopold von Ranke. In him Baeck found a pious striving for righteousness, 'letting both sides approach him'. Ranke could call the nations 'God's ideas'. Here one comes close to the biblical text in which the divine plan is evident in everything. Hans Liebeschütz connects Baeck with Ranke:

> ...the juxtaposition of Bible, antiquity and Germanhood which Western culture represented for him was for Ranke a work of art and a symbol of the divine providence behind earthly phenomena... and Baeck saw in the world of the ideas of the Berlin historian the living activity of the prophetic interpretation of world history, from which he also derived his own interpretation of the destiny and task of the Jewish people (Introduction to L. Baeck, *Aus drei Jahrtausenden*, Tübingen 1958, 6).

It was his bond with the honesty, the decency and the profundity of thought in German culture which made it possible for Leo Baeck to revisit Germany after the war. His experiences in the 1920s, his encounters in the time of the Weimar Republic, also smoothed Baeck's way back to his brothers. He could no longer live in Germany: London, Cincinnati and Jerusalem were now his home. But his teaching built and still builds bridges, by which we approached ourselves during this semester.

A new edition of my book on Leo Baeck is being published in 1990, so it is unnecessary to go more deeply into this theme here. However, I must say that the students in Wuppertal were intensely sympathetic to the topic of Leo Baeck, to an extraordinary degree, above all to the two books *The Essence of Judaism* and *This People Israel*. The formulation of an ethical way of life which associated the best of Immanuel Kant with the ethical rigorism of the rabbis of the first century proved stimulating reading. It convinced me that this journey really was a highpoint of my life – and that Leo Baeck would continue to remain as a guest in the students' rooms.

Much about Leo Baeck fascinated the students. There was the fact that he could hold so many offices in the 1920s: President of the General Association of German Rabbis; Grand President of the B'nai B'rith order; President of Keren Hayessod and a member of the committee of the Jewish Agency; and, at the same time, a member of the non-Zionist Central Association of German Citizens of Jewish Faith; in the National Federation of Jewish Frontline Soldiers; while simultaneously being a leader of Jewish pacifism. How could one live with these contradictions and at the same time be a pastor, a rabbi of German Jewry? We read his article on positive neutrality, but much about Baeck still remained a mystery. The ten two-hour sessions which I devoted to this topic were not enough time – one never has enough time.

Without Bertold Klappert I could never have done my work; he was a real partner. Only at one point did I leave him in the lurch: I refused to join the football team which won a great victory over the students (many of whom were female). There I disgraced myself: the saying went the rounds that the rabbi loved the old tradition and was very upset that the teams did not exchange shirts after the games.

It was also Bertold who brought me to the Landesvater, and again I was not the worthy rabbi whom Professor Klappert wanted to introduce to Landesvater Johannes Rau. We visited him in his home; it was a friendly, pleasant time. Only at the beginning and the end of the visit did I make my mistakes. Rau asked me, 'Well, rabbi, what do you want of me? A gift of money?' 'Nothing at all,' I replied. 'Impossible. Everyone wants something of me.' 'Give me ten minutes and I'll think of something,' I said.

Then we talked on questions of Christian-Jewish collaboration. I found Herr Rau a deeply pious, completely open Christian, with whom I could also talk about the past. His recollections of the Jews in his youth, of 'Kristallnacht' and the temptations that any respectable person had to fight against at that time, were a topic which brought us together. We also spoke of the hope of establishing many teaching posts for Judaism in the colleges of his Land, and here I left the talking to Bertold. He knew what could be and had to be achieved. And he also reminded Johannes Rau of a visit they had paid together to Jerusalem. Rau also gave funds to institutions for Christian-Jewish collaboration and was enthused by the work.

We talked on and on, and it grew dark. Finally I got up – how discourteous can one be? – and said energetically, 'Herr Rau, my plane to London leaves in fifty minutes. I must say good-bye.' We laughed and parted. I knew that it was now impossible to get to the airport in time. But one has to try, and so I arrived precisely at the flight time. I found an angry group of passengers: two hours delay! My cheerful reception of this news made me somewhat unpopular with my fellow-passengers. I telephoned to convince Bertold that I had special influence over the transcendent.

He just said, 'You're lucky.' And that's true. The luck of having such colleagues made it possible for me to overcome the inhibitions of my youth and to go forward on the journey towards reconciliation.

But the road is long, and the world is cold and dark...

A Conversation in the German Forest

It was a magical house, deep in the forest. At break of day the wagtails came and knocked on the bedroom window. They always did that, every morning, but I was the guest, so they came to me. I looked out of the window. A hare was running round the house through the grass. The grace at meals was sincere and simple. Good people lived here.

'Can you see the cross up there on the hill?' Heinrich asked me when he picked me up from Bebra station. 'That's the memorial cross for Adam.' 'Is it the only one?' 'In fact it is. After they hanged him, his ashes were scattered. The family tomb is here. A year ago, after a great fight in the community, his name was put on the roll of honour in the church – there it does not even say "they died for the Fatherland". Elisabeth still believes that he was entitled to his own plate. But this community...'

Heinrich von Trott zu Solz, brother of Adam, one of the 'conspirators' against Hitler, who was involved in the preparations for the attempt on his life on 20 July 1944, met me for the first time in Berlin, on 20 July 1984, when I gave the opening address at the ceremony commemorating the resistance. Then he came to my Rosenzweig lecture in Kassel and the Moltke family brought me to this house. At the time there was snow on the forest and the house. We sat together by the fireside in the living room and talked about the past. Now I had come by myself, 'in the lovely month of May'. Already I had become one of the friends of the family, of whom there were many, who saw the peaceful house in the forest as a refuge from the restless, loud world.

'It's because we're so close to the frontier,' said Heinrich, 'there are no jet fighters in the air. And there's no traffic on the roads, the area's a poor one. Only the forest. Here you get close to nature. You can hear and understand yourself. And you can reflect on personal relationships.'

Heinrich looked at me with concern. 'How are you? Isn't it difficult for you to spend a long time in Germany?'

It was difficult. This was the first time for forty years that I had declared my readiness to live in Germany for four months. The old problems, the fear of the dark time, had revived in me. In London I could talk about these problems without difficulty; there the problem of 'Forgive and Forget' was a theoretical theological question which I could discuss in the columns of the London *Times*, in my journal *European Judaism*, or at scholarly conferences. But here it was not a theory but again an existential experience. And I was lonely. Bertold Klappert and Siegbard Kunath in Wuppertal supported me; they understood, had proved their worth. But where were the other conversation partners?

In the forest of the brothers Grimm, a few miles away, I recalled some of their cruel stories. And here I had to ask myself: forgive or forget?

In the terminology of my opponents in England these terms were chock-full of prejudice: hatred was said to be making itself heard, the grim intensity of the wounded, whose suffering gave no rest, whose anger still kept breaking out against the sinners and the grandchildren of the sinners. How could I convince them that my position did not arise out of anger, out of a feeling of vengeance? How could I prove to them that forgetting would destroy the world, that a one-sided forgiveness on my side would only be a meaningless word, which any germ of emerging repentance from the other side would throttle?

Heinrich von Trott zu Solz understood this. Fifty years previously, on 'Kristallnacht', he had been living near Freiburg im Breisgau. There was no synagogue in the area; only one Jewish family was living there. The young man went to them. 'I shall spend tonight here,' he said. 'Perhaps I can help.' And the police came during the night, were amazed to see him – and nothing happened.

'Much changed for me during that night,' he said, 'it became a key experience in my life.' The same year he had got to know Wilfried Israel from Berlin, and the tragic existence of the Jews had become real to him. The rich department-store owner had recognized the young man as a true conversation partner – and had opened up to him. 'Only in this time of suffering could I find my way back to my faith and the religion of my fathers,' he declared to Heinrich, who was twenty at the time. Perhaps it was this meeting which led him to his Jewish fellow human beings on 'Kristallnacht'.

We again sat by the fireside, together with his son Levin and wife Elisabeth. She was younger, but she too remembered the time in their small village. On the Saturday Jews would come through the village on their way to the synagogue in a larger village. They were friendly, would stop and chat with the children. 'And then they suddenly disappeared,' said Elisabeth. Many Germans have such memories, but only a few drew the consequences with the intensity and the moral indignation of this family, which was involved in the resistance against Hitler. Heinrich told me of a new book in which Adam's letters had been made public.

'Of course it also shows weak points in his life,' he said. 'No one is perfect. But Adam's death proves something, gives a final answer to the question that was put to him.'

We talked about Martin Niemöller, about Dietrich Bonhoeffer, and about the question of the limited support for the Jews, about the constraints with which Christian doctrines had weakened courage to show solidarity with them. Heinrich saw this very clearly; he was sharp in his criticism and we agreed that one cannot sum up a life from one particular moment.

In the afternoon we went into the forest again. Woodcutters were at work, and Heinrich was the forester in his forest. The men were Yugoslavs, industrious and energetic, and had a good relationship with Heinrich. The rotten wood at the end of a branch has to be sawn off, is worthless. But instead of simply sawing off three or four metres, as many do, these men sawed off less, examined it, and so saved more of the valuable wood. Heinrich showed me the difference between pine and spruce, lime and other trees in the wood. He knew every tree and marked those which were now ready for felling. We went deeper into the forest, through a fence.

'Deer once broke in here,' he showed me. 'They destroyed all these trees by gnawing at the bark'. We came to a great bald patch in the forest, where only a few very small spruce trees were slowly attempting a new beginning. 'Deer?' I asked. Heinrich laughed. 'No.' The weather had turned bad: first rain, then snow, then a sudden cold which suddenly brought the thermometer from five degrees above zero to ten degrees below. Spruce and pine had snow on their branches, which became heavy ice. They all fell, the spruce and the firs. But limes lose their leaves in the winter; they bow to the storm – and survive.

'Can one apply this lesson to human beings?' I asked. 'Certainly,' said Heinrich, and then reflected. 'Not always, of course, if we're now thinking about the past. To bow in order to survive brings its own dangers. But then I have to remember my father-in-law, a simple man in a village. He recognized the Hitler danger straight away, and it did not destroy him. But the great professors, the giants – they all fell before the Hitler storm. The whole of society collapsed.'

And then Heinrich von Trott told me something of his family history, so that in a German forest I could understand more of the tragedy of the German people, to take it into my own life.

I had already admired the bronze bust of his father, this Wilhelmine face. The original once stood in the Kultusminister-ium, since he was in fact Minister of Culture. As Heinrich told the story, he was firmly loyal: emperor and church were one for him. Much changed after the war, and he didn't like it, but he could not change; he remained conservative. He gave Heinrich the choice of becoming an officer or a civil servant. But Heinrich refused: he wanted to be a farmer. Impossible! With misgivings his father then allowed him to train as a forester. His father died at a ripe old age in 1938, and so was spared much. He could not see the future, would not have been able to understand how his old, worthy house had had to oppose developments in Germany. One son became a Communist, one was executed as a traitor, a third became a deserter – and in each case the decision that the sons made was moral and correct. How could he have understood something like this? Could he have seen it as a continuation of the history of the Trott zu Solz family?

Heinrich was then conscripted into the Wehrmacht and served on the Soviet front. Then he was sent – by Adam – into the 'Indian army', to France (a stupid propaganda affair). It was 1944 when the command came to attack the Maquis. Heinrich refused, and told his group that an order from Hitler was nothing compared to the voice of his own conscience. Thirty soldiers, the chaplain and the doctor followed him and deserted. It was the day on which Adam was hanged – but he did not know that. The Germans attempted to capture him and also told his mother that everyone had been captured and hanged. But they had surrendered to the Maquis. They were taken through the ruins of Oradour, shut up in a stable, and then arrived at a prison in Poitiers, in which SS and other prisoners were also awaiting their fate. A group of hostile Maquis came and called for all the officers, the SS and the 'Indians'. Heinrich, the chaplain and the doctor were rescued by the commandant; the rest were all shot.

The three were then taken together to a large prison. In rags, without badges of rank, they stumbled into a group which had just been informed by a captured general that Rundstedt had 'won'. Victory! They said to Heinrich: 'Someone like you is already lying under the boards of our hut. Your turn will come!' The Polish guards couldn't care less, and his life was again in danger. So he was subjected to a 'Germanic' Christmas, with bits of the Edda, stupid quotations and folkish songs. But on New Year's Day an American came who knew Adam von Trott. Soon after that Heinrich was on a liberty ship on the way to an English prison. After a variety of camps he ended up at Ascot, where the real anti-Nazis were finally brought together. Sir Stafford Cripps visited him, and David Astor. A new life began, with mourning for his friends of the 20th of July, and mourning for Germany. He came home and built his house in the forest. He did not want to leave it again – nor had he.

Heinrich showed me a green Douglas fir from America standing next to a beautiful red fir. The fragrance brought us back to the world of nature, to a holy stillness, in which one could find the way back to oneself. Could our shared suffering also bring our families together?

Something had already united us for years: a love of Paul Celan. Heinrich wanted to hear every word that Paul had once said to me. He himself had read everything that had been written about Celan, and knew more than forty poems by heart. 'Someone asked Celan about the meaning of a poem,' Heinrich said to me, 'and Celan simply said that one had to read and read any poem until one understood it. I now understand those poems that I know by heart. And behind each poem I hear the darkness that pursued him and found him. I hear the grief and mourning for his family who died, the grief and the feeling of guilt because he did not die. At night, when I can't sleep, I say these poems to myself. Perhaps...' he looked at me, 'perhaps I'm also learning the poems out of anxiety about a time when I no longer have any books, against a time of blindness.'

And so we came out of the forest.

'There on the field, that's a deer – perhaps two,' he showed me. We were walking along the edge of the forest.

'I want to tell you another terrible thing, because it's about your country, America,' he said. 'In the time of the empire one of my distant relatives founded the Kaiser Wilhelm Research Institute. Later it became an institute for race studies, and even later it sent Dr Mengele to Auschwitz to continue his investigations into twins. You know the story. But yesterday I heard that there is now a dispute in America as to whether the results may not be usable – in the end science is neutral, and the results could be used. How can something like that be used? How can anyone think of such a thing?' I agreed, and then spoke of the difficulties for a country trying to find the way to the ideals of its foundation. But Heinrich had hope for the USA. 'Vietnam changed a lot of things,' he thought, 'and I really believe that new ideas about war and peace and about the way forward to the future for America are developing. I must also say that I have similar hopes for Germany. A generation has been lost. And the generation between thirty-five and sixty-five has succumbed to the economic miracle. They work, build a new existence for themselves, and want to

41

forget eveything. I really do believe in the forty years in the wilderness, in the dying out of the generation. But the twenty-year-olds today are different. I have hope.'

We spoke about Schleswig-Holstein – how could one have avoided it on this election day? The German 'Watergate' would certainly bring a new party to power in that Land, the Social Democrats. In Heinrich's view the 'sinner' Barschel was far worse than Nixon. 'Even in his youth, it was said, he had to be first. And if anyone proved better, he slandered him and got rid of him. And so he had never changed... but these days the voters have changed,' Heinrich thought.

On the last day we were sitting together again. We came to the questions which are addressed to the people of Israel out of simple piety. 'What about the Messiah?' he wanted to know. 'Is he only for the Jews? Is there a resurrection for all? Is there paradise?' We looked at the different possibilities in Jewish belief, how the kingdom of God is to be realized in this world; we spoke about secular messianism, which can show itself as Zionism or socialism. Jews live wholly in this world. Heinrich was impressed that they still have hope for humanity.

'But what about evil?' he asked. And so we arrived at the old question of human freedom, and also agreed that evil has a life of its own outside our understanding. I would not allow him Job's Satan – he was only a state attorney with duties in the heavenly court. And we also had to reject Ahriman in Persian dualism: belief in the one God does not allow any power alongside him. Evil, this *tremendum* of the dark that we always only touch on and can never understand, remains in the world like the ashes of Auschwitz. Does God also remain in the world? Some people doubt it.

'Could Adolf Hitler get to heaven?' was the next question to me and Judaism, simple and honest.

I wasn't prepared for it. In our conversation about the resurrection I had mentioned the old dispute between Pharisees and Sadducees, this misunderstood group of Pharisees, who wanted to fight for the people and defended belief in the resurrection against the attack of the Sadducees. The latter did not have the possibility of resurrection (they did not even believe in it), but 'the righteous of all nations have their share

in the resurrection'. Now if resurrection is a human concept,
then one must allow it for everyone. But Hitler? We had already
agreed that we did not believe in hell – only in so far as one can
see this hell on earth. But Hitler in heaven?

'You know,' I said to Heinrich, 'evil lives in the world and
goes on living there. The poison of the Hitler period is still
everywhere. So "Hitler in heaven" is a thought that Jews
cannot express simply because it would give this demonic a
kind of legitimation in the world. Let's get back to the question
of retribution and forgiveness. "Death atones for all" is an
important Jewish doctrine. Hitler is now subject to divine
judgment, not human judgment. We would not dare, like
some Christian theologians, to proclaim God's thoughts and
judgment, to relate it to individual cases and thus to promise
forgiveness to Hitler, to Eichmann or to the hangman of
Treblinka. There we hold back. Repentance remains the beginning of a change of mind, the way to the time of forgiveness.
God is the righteous, merciful judge.'

'Yes,' said Heinrich, 'I agree. But there is also a forgiveness,
a reconciliation, between peoples. Now, after Auschwitz, I
keep thinking how much Christian doctrine has to change. We
hear so often that the Jews killed our saviour, that they live
under eternal punishment. As if it was not humankind, we
ourselves, who killed Jesus. And then we killed the Jews.
So when people say, "Jesus died on the cross", one must
immediately add, "and the Jews died in Auschwitz". We must
now see our Christianity in quite a different light. Never again
may we accuse the Jewish people of murdering God.'

I thought of Friedel Marquardt and our meeting at the
Nuremberg Kirchentag in 1979. We were giving a report on
faith and life after Auschwitz, and his Christian and my Jewish
attempt came together in the valley of death. This was the first
stage on a way which takes us ever further. Here in the forest
I heard the same thing from a simple, good man, who had
never studied, but whose library contained the wisdom of the
world. He expressed his own experience, his own suffering.
But in the long winter nights, in his encounter with philo-
sophers, theologians and therapists, the truth of his experience
became stronger. In the evening I had been looking for some-

thing in the library and had seen Plato, Hegel, Schelling, Heidegger and the rest. I opened a book on Heidegger: '…we always called her "the green one", because Hannah Arendt always wore this dress,' and I remembered her, but not in green. Hegel's *The State* – Adam von Trott had written his name in it. Books on depth psychology, on evil… Could I understand Heinrich von Trott zu Solz through his books? My beloved scholar Zunz had composed the biography of Rashi from his quotations of books. But Heinrich von Trott was not to be found in the books, but in life, in his love, in his forest.

Elie Wiesel tells the story of the great Baal Shem Tov, who went into the forest, to a particular place, to bring about the redemption of his people with special prayers. His pupil went into the forest, as he did, but no longer knew the place where the master had lit his little fire to say his prayer. But he still knew the prayer and so brought redemption. His pupil did not even know the prayer, but he went into the forest, and that was enough. 'Today,' says Elie Wiesel, 'today we only know the story. That must be enough – God loves stories.'

But I now know a place in the forest where I can meet a fellow human being. Perhaps that is a beginning. It must not be an end.

Martin Niemöller and the Jewish Cemetery

In a travel guide to the Tecklenburger Land Martin Niemöller tells how as a boy he could shorten the journey from Westerkappeln to Wersen by going through the beautiful old forest cemetery of the Jewish community. The firs and the pines made a chapel, a place of silence, and he went that way with quiet joy. A Catholic lady, Frau Althoff from Rheine, read this passage, went there, and began a work on the history of this Jewish community which grew into a large and well-received book. Now I had come to visit Niemöller's tomb and to travel the short distance from there to this Jewish cemetery.

I was not alone. Sybil Niemöller von Zell, Martin's partner in the last decade of his activities, went with me, along with Pastor Beck. I had wanted to come here the previous year, after a conference in Loccum with Elie Wiesel. But I had to return to my congregation in London, and so at that time Sybil took Elie to this place of recollection and reflection. Now I was there, and there was much to think about.

First of all, this place and this community. Martin Niemöller wanted to be buried here, in his homeland, where his ancestors had already found their resting place. The church would have preferred Wiesbaden, where more visitors would come to the memorial. When Sybil respected the dead man's last wish, an offer was made of a great monument in Wersen, by one of the best artists, because the cemetery was felt to be very modest. But Sybil refused. The tombstone was cut by the village stonemason — large, but simple, just right for Martin Niemöller and for this cemetery. And right for the community? That is questionable. The community had refused to make Martin Niemöller an honorary citizen. Some people said that he had fouled the nest. And one has to remember that in this district Adolf Hitler got the highest percentage of votes – it was not until 1986 that a memorial could be put up for Jewish fellow citizens who died in the concentration camps.

On the other hand Pastor Beck could really call himself a friend and pupil of Martin Niemöller, and his home was often a secure, peaceful lodging for his old teacher. Moreover the parish house, 'Martin Niemöller House', was built by many members of the Westerkappeln community with their own hands as a reply to the Wersen rejection of Niemöller. The three of us went into this building and I saw working groups preparing for a trip to Israel. The theology courses in the Martin Niemöller House not only covered themes like '400 years of the Heidelberg Catechism in the Tecklenburger Land' or 'Suddenly alone – after death', but also 'Mass unemployment and permanent unemployment, a challenge to the church', and 'A history of antisemitism up to the Holocaust'. Here a deepening of the spirit and of community life was called for: further development, reflection of the kind that had also been found in the life of Martin Niemöller.

Sybil played a cassette on the car radio, a BBC broadcast on Martin Niemöller that Paul Oestreicher had made. There was much in this broadcast that brought Niemöller home to me. Niemöller had found it too uncritical, Sybil said, although Paul had described both the angry disputatious fighter for the church and the genial friend and pastor. It is certain that Niemöller was slow to recognize the Hitler danger, and also that his patriotic fervour was so ardent that he did not see many fearful things along the way. But that he was Hitler's prisoner from 1937 to 1945, that he trod the way of suffering from prison to Sachsenhausen and to Dachau, offers us other perspectives on his life. He himself came to a recognition of guilt and a confession of guilt which – in contrast to others – applied in the first place to himself. He spoke not only of the mistakes of his generation, but of his own sins in failing to act, failing to see, failing to understand.

It is difficult for a rabbi to put himself into this career and into these thoughts, to develop empathy and sympathy for a life which is so important for the understanding of a whole world. Was it ever my world? Sybil told me much of her world – a world of generals and the aristocracy, of the religious and intellectual repudiation of Fascism, coupled with her own tragedy and experiences, the darkness in the brightness, and also the good in the evil. When she was allowed to bring food parcels to her father in prison, there was an SS man who told her and others to bring more bread – there were prisoners who had no relatives. Even the fight within the family between anti-Fascists and those who believed in Hitler belonged in a world which was far removed from my own. The child who worshipped the Führer as a seven-year-old and then – in the family tradition – turned against him, fell in love with the pastor Martin Niemöller. This love was fulfilled after a long, long time. The stations of this road were difficult. How could I understand all this?

At the Jewish cemetery the tombstones stood in orderly rows, quite undisturbed. Only time had removed a few letters. But the visitors found a complete German text. One had to go round the stones to find the Hebrew writing on the other side. Was the life of this community like this, outwardly adapted but nevertheless preserving the distinctive, the particular? Two tombs opposite each other bore the same name: the small grandchild and the grandmother had died at almost the same time. The new memorial towered above all the other tombstones. No stone lay on any tombstone – there were no descendants here to visit their family and leave behind a small stone as a token of their visit. The forest was there. History. The past. I said the prayer '*El mole rachamim*', Lord of mercy.

We returned to the pastor's house.

As in many homes of thoughtful people, I found a mass of books not just about Christianity and its development in time, including its Jewish roots, but also about Judaism itself, testimonies to the faith of Jewish teachers. Herr Beck had heard something of Leo Baeck, and had an understanding of a common heritage which embraced not only the biblical period but also the development of Germany from the Reformation up to the present day. And he had inherited his teacher Niesel's library, which included works by Martin Niemöller, many with a personal dedication. Then he also brought us a book of

Dietrich Bonhoeffer's (*The Cost of Discipleship*) signed by the author. There was a short letter, addressed to Professor Niesel. Bonhoeffer thanked him for his criticism of the book – but it was too short; the reviewer should read the book again and would find much more in it.

We had to return. Sybil told me that I had given the same verdict as Martin Niemöller: Frau Beck's soup was fabulous. But I had added that the Rote Grütze was also extraordinary: as good as in the best restaurants in Hamburg, where this is a speciality. In theological questions I am often uncertain in my judgments, on gastronomic matters never – there, our two worlds reunite.

One of Niemöller's books describes the way from the U-boat to the pulpit. That reminded me of an encounter which I had had less than twenty-four hours before this visit, with the Kamikaze pilot who became a disciple of Bonhoeffer.

The Kamikaze Pilot,
Dietrich Bonhoeffer and
Chanina Ben Teradion

The American television serial 'Cheers' features Woody, a wide-eyed, innocent bartender. In one episode, Woody speculates upon the nature of Kamikaze pilots.

'I'd love to meet one of them some day,' he says. 'Boy, the tales these guys have to tell!'

His friends view him kindly, unwilling to break the news to him that a Kamikaze pilot, trained to perform one suicide mission, will not be available for future interviews.

I met a Kamikaze pilot recently, and he did have quite a tale to tell. He was a 'failed' Kamikaze pilot, of course, but it was not his fault. Trained to perfection for the performance of that task, towards the end of World War II, he had reported for duty – only to be overtaken by the end of the war. For a long time he wrestled within his soul, somehow unfulfilled, uncertain whether to live or to die. Finally, a great change occurred within him, and he became a devout Christian. He became a disciple of one of the great martyrs of twentieth-century Christianity, Dietrich Bonhoeffer. The former pilot translated Bonhoeffer's works into Japanese and, when I met him, he had become an outstanding teacher of Christianity in the Eastern and Western world.

We met in Amsterdam, that city of many encounters. The great International Bonhoeffer Conference of 1988 was about to take place, and I had come from Wuppertal to give a paper on Bonhoeffer and the Jews. In my customary fashion, I had written nothing in my diary except 'Amsterdam/Bonhoeffer'. I arrived at Schiphol airport and cheerfully telephoned the local Reform rabbi David Lilienthal, who had once been my student in London.

'Find me the time, the place, and my hotel,' I enjoined him, 'otherwise I'll be your guest!' His martyred sigh indicated that he had not forgotten my casual approach to life. Galvanized into action by my threat, he called back in fifteen minutes with the name of my hotel. There, my arrival was greeted with mixed feelings. The conference programme was so tight, with so many scholars denied the opportunity of lecturing, that my late arrival had already prompted three professors to offer themselves modestly as my replacement. But I *wanted* to give this paper, since the problem of Bonhoeffer and the Jews had troubled me for many years. Here was a great man, rightly honoured and appreciated for his stand against Hitler, murdered in the end by an evil state which recognized his absolute challenge as a voice of religious conscience speaking out against the Nazis and on behalf of the Jews. But had Bonhoeffer been consistent in this fight against evil from the very beginning? Had he not faltered initially; more, had his Christian doctrine not set him against the Jews in some ways? For the new disciples, like my Japanese pilot, Bonhoeffer was perfect, a knight in shining armour. Others saw flaws in the man and in his teachings.

Personally I prefer flawed saints – they offer far more hope to the individual who knows that perfection lies outside one's own grasp, and welcomes a knight who can sometimes come a cropper. In my midrash lecture in Wuppertal I had picked out the person of Noah, described in the Bible as 'a righteous man in his time'. Bonhoeffer – even if we see imperfections in his person and his teachings – gives us a vibrant testimony to the goodness of the Christian who fights evil and shows compassion to his neighbours.

In 1933 Bonhoeffer reached three conclusions regarding the Christian church and its relationship to the German state. It could and should criticize the state for acting in an immoral fashion. It could and should help the victims of oppression, suffering and tortured by that state. It could, but should not, enter into full rebellion against such a state (Luther's obedience to the state was still strong in Bonhoeffer). When the state threw all Christians of Jewish descent out of the church, Bonhoeffer fought against this and for 'his' Jews. Later...

later... he fought for all Jews. 'We Christians resisted by confessing, but we did not confess by resisting,' says Eberhard Bethge in assessing Bonhoeffer and the Christian response to the Nazis. But in the end, the kingdom of heaven is won by one action, whether sooner or later. And a theology purges itself when it can say, as does Bonhoeffer, 'The Jew keeps open the question of Christ.' At that point, the totally committed Christian comes to recognize that a continuing challenge to that faith cannot be ignored, nor removed through human violence, nor disposed of by 'divine plan'. The published proceedings of that conference continue the theme; and I went back to Wuppertal, richer through that encounter with Christianity and the pilot. And, on the train, I encountered a pacifist to match the former warrior.

We were alone in a compartment on the way to Düsseldorf. He was a young German student who had opted for community service as the alternative to military training; and he planned to study theology. When he discovered that I had just attended a Dietrich Bonhoeffer Conference in Amsterdam he abandoned all reserve: Who was I? And what was I?

The moment of decision comes very early in this type of encounter with a stranger. One can withdraw; one can hide from the other or discourage him or her through rudeness. And one can enter into immediate confrontation which can enlarge or diminish the identities of the other and of oneself.

'*Ivri Anochi* – I am a Jew,' I said with Jonah. 'I am a rabbi. And I've been speaking about Bonhoeffer's role in the resistance against Hitler.'

We covered much ground in the next three hours. Part of our conversation could be classified as inter-faith dialogue. But there were awkward passages in which we confronted ourselves as German and Jewish; there were long moments of silence. And there were explorations in the field of philosophy and history where we had to find compatible standards of judgment. What did our religious traditions have to say about the righteous person who is stricken by apathy and does not stand against evil in a dark time? Or the flawed human being who at some moment in life rises above himself and saves a life? My Christian friend believed in death-bed repentance and declared, 'One can attain paradise in one moment of repentance.'

I experienced a shock of recognition then, and quoted the words of a second-century rabbi, R.Judah ha-Nasi: 'There are those who gain eternal life in an hour, while others strive to attain it for many years!'

And then I felt it incumbent upon me to tell him the story of Chanina ben Teradion and his executioner. Hans Christoph – my companion on the train – had used the example of priests who entered the concentration camps of their own free will, and of the rare camp guards who secretly tried to help some of the inmates. Perhaps some of the stories were the stuff of legend and the hope that someone like that had existed. And, perhaps for that reason, this story was true and had to be true. After all, the midrash of ben Teradion and his executioner is such a legend - and must therefore be true. We *must* hope in the goodness of others, particularly in the darkest of times. And perhaps the dialogue recorded in the Midrash took place then and 1800 years later, in the camps where death waited and the hangman was a master from Germany. Only those who were there can report if conversations across the abyss took place here. But the ancient tale I retold on the train has a quality of authenticity within it: behind the facts (?) one can feel the anguished reaching-out towards the neighbour. And that there were Romans who responded in this manner to the anguish of the Jews is attested through the conversions to Judaism which did not cease in that dark time.

Here is the story:

Rabbi Chanina ben Teradion continued to teach the Torah against the Roman edict which had tried to stamp out Judaism, as it had destroyed the Temple and Jerusalem in that fearful time. He was caught with the Torah scroll across his lap, teaching it to many students. The Romans took him, wrapped him in his Torah scroll, tied him to the stake, heaped faggots around him, and lit the fire. But they soaked cotton and woollen cloths with water and tied them to his breast so that he would not die quickly. His daughter cried out, 'O father, to see you like this!' But he replied, 'How painful it would be to die in the flames, were it not for the Torah burning with me! God will avenge this injury to the holy word, and I will be included in his concern.'

His students asked, 'Rabbi, what do you see?' He answered: 'I see the parts of parchment consumed by the fire - but the letters of the text fly upwards!' Then they said, 'Rabbi, open your mouth wide so that the flames can enter and you can die quickly!' But he replied: 'He who has given the soul will take it – but no one should assist in surrendering to death.'

At this point, the executioner spoke up: 'Rabbi, if I build up the fire even more, and remove the material soaked with water from your breast – will you take me with you into life eternal?' The martyr said, 'I will'. 'Give me your oath on it,' said the Roman, and the rabbi did so. The executioner made the fire stronger, removed the wet woollen protection from the rabbi's body, and Chanina ben Teradion's soul left his body. Then the Roman jumped into the fire and died in turn. A heavenly voice then proclaimed: 'Chanina ben Teradion and the Roman executioner both have their share in eternal life.'

Rabbi Judah ha-Nasi's comment refers to this specific event. There is another version of the story in which Chanina waits for an hour to consider whether or not he should swallow the flames and die quickly, and a longer conversation takes place between the rabbi and his executioner. Chanina even points out that God has other ways of bringing death: bears, leopards, lions, wolves, or snakes and scorpions – God only uses the Romans as his tool in a plan humans cannot begin to comprehend. And, in that variant, the Roman executioner jumps into the fire with the rabbi, ready to accept either life or death according to the divine will.

It grew dark in our compartment, on those Bundesbahn rails which had been traversed by other trains leading to cities of life and death, to fires burning through the night. Hans Christoph wanted to know more about Chanina ben Teradion and his fate; but there were too many stories, too many parallels to modern times: of the daughter made a Feldhure (placed in a house of prostitution) because of her beauty, of the son who had rebelled against his father's teachings, of Chanina's colleagues... they enter the liturgies of Judaism as the 'Ten Martyrs' and are recalled on special occasions during the year. The fact remained that we could not follow them into that darkness. Standing outside the circle of hell, Hans Christoph and I could engage in a religious dialogue, as Christian and Jew, where our personal problems were shared and where respect for the other tradition grew. And we could only wonder whether there was dialogue in that dark hell outside our experience. Separated from others, was there nevertheless dialogue between the sufferers of different traditions? And – a strange thought to contemplate, but enforced by the stories about Ben Teradion and the Roman executioner – did *such* encounters take place in the darkness which touched upon our own lives within this century of brutality?

On that train, we only gave each other our first names: a greater intimacy, a greater distance. Some other time, some other journey, may bring us together to confirm or to deny the reality of that encounter. Meanwhile, I think more often of Bonhoeffer, and of Lichtenberg. Perhaps Hans Christoph searches in his mind – what was the name of that rabbi in Roman times? Yet I am certain that he sees the letters flying upward from the Torah, and that he remembers the unnamed executioner.

The Sayings of the Fathers and Lenin

Again we were in the German forest, deep in conversation. But things were quite different. Why? 'Ask Lenin.'

'That's the Bismarck oak,' someone explained to me, 'every wood has one.' But in the next clearing there was something quite different: large, massive black granite, which tried in vain to approach the tops of the fir trees. It was already getting dark, but I could recognize the profile chiselled above, even without reading the name below it: Lenin. Why? The way to the Finland station never really led through the beechwood of Templin, eighty miles from Berlin, in the DDR. But his ideas and teachings had gone through the country, and the pastors accompanying me through the wood were well aware of this.

'At the end of the wood is a recreation centre for party members,' one of them told me. 'But in fact everyone is invited to take a summer study course on Marxist teaching. I registered a couple of years ago. They wouldn't believe it. "You? Seriously?" I said yes. "But in what category can we put you? No, it's impossible. You would be a disruptive influence." So I couldn't go on the course.'

We came to the end of the wood. A car was standing there. 'Do you have a permit?' someone asked me. It was the police. Of course I had my passport and visa in my pocket – I was still very aware of the difficulties I had had in getting it, though this time the church and not the state had made the mistake. The pastoral college had invited me to come for three days of lectures and Bible study with the clergy, and they had only applied for one day, so they hadn't got the right visa. A long line stood on Friedrichstrasse waiting to get from West Berlin to East Berlin. But as usual I had arranged 'protection'. A former confirmand, Jon Greenwald, was the head of the political section of the American embassy in East Berlin. His wife met me in a car with diplomatic plates and in a couple of minutes took me through Checkpoint Charlie. But I had had to register the visa in Templin, and after some hesitation and waiting it was extended for a day. I didn't have to show it in the forest, but the police were looking at us mistrustfully. Why were we standing by the Lenin monument? That was not prohibited. But – we had been laughing.

The 'pastors' school' was in the Waldhof, a house in the midst of a hospital area for over 300 mentally ill, handicapped children, women and men, who were receiving very considerate treatment. There was agricultural work as therapy, and work in the forest. But we were also surrounded by children at play. The food was simple; they had arranged a cheese-plate for me. The work was taken seriously. Hardly had I arrived than the group sat round the table to be instructed. Horst had brought me from Berlin – in great anxiety, as he said, since he had never met a rabbi before. He took a detour to show me the house in which the Jewish doctor had lived who looked after him and his family before the war. He also gave me thirty questions which had already been compiled by the group and which I was to answer. Pastor Johannes Hildebrandt of the Sophienkirche in Berlin had already spent a day with them discussing the problem of anti-Judaism in Christian teaching. The questions which I was given in the car related only to theological problems. By the time we arrived I had sorted the questions, and I expressed delight at the admirably rapid drive. 'That's good,' said Horst Kastner, 'in fact I have only one eye.' I thanked him again, for not telling me this at the beginning of the drive. Then we went in.

In the next two days it became clear to me how important this dialogue was for the group. In fact one could hardly call it dialogue; it was more a period of enlightenment. Some were locked up in old theological positions and attacked the liberal thought of Hildebrandt and Kastner. Others were afraid of me: would a Jew challenge their right to preach? Would he attack the figure of Jesus? But they had come. They were prepared to listen, so this was not to be a disputation, but instruction. Some of the questions showed where they stood and what inhibitions there were:

In your view, can the Decalogue as a gift and help to life be reconciled with its use as a penitential model?

Is it necessary to acknowledge the children of Abraham in faith without anxiety and accusation?

Can we read the prophets together in their criticism of the people of God (and of humankind)?

What is the Jewish understanding of Jeremiah 31.31-34 (the 'new covenant')?

What expectations does a Jew have of Bible readers who are not Jews?

Can one separate being a Jew from belief in God (do atheists belong to the Jewish people)?

Where are the beginnings of Christian-Jewish dialogue after 1945? Are Christians seeking dialogue to carry on mission? Are Jews seeking dialogue to 'bring Jesus home'?

This last question touched on a theme that Johannes Hildebrandt had already discussed with them. But I was very much aware that many in this group were lonely pastors who laboriously had to look after three or four villages under the pressure of a government which was not very well disposed to religion and who lived in very different conditions from their colleagues on the other side of the 'wall'. The conversation with Jews had hardly begun – in a world in which they had no conversation partners. Some were a long way on and became impatient; they had read a great deal, went regularly to the Jewish service in Berlin, had learned Hebrew and lived wholly for dialogue. Someone who had visited Israel had had to struggle with the temptation to go over to Judaism. In the end it made him a deeper, more believing Christian. Here I had to be careful; I could not detach him from the group and draw him 'on to my side'. We had to become one group. I was not here to win debating points, to crush each carefully expressed attack. Slowly, cautiously, I went from one question to another.

What they saw as an introduction to the Ten Commandments – 'I am the Lord, your God, who led you out of Egypt, from the house of slavery' – became a long excursus in which I showed them that this was the first of the ten words, an introduction to the faith which cannot see this teaching as a 'penitential model'. In the saying on the sabbath they had to recognize the whole creation and hear of the great freedom which must lead to social justice. The sabbath as a momentary enjoyment of the messianic time to come was also strange to them. The word of God stood before them as a complete revelation, and it took some time for them to understand that for us the commentaries of rabbis and scribes, the 'oral Torah', are part of the same revelation. They had almost more understanding for Zoroastrian thought, in which each letter conveys an eternal truth; the mysticism in Judaism could be compared with mystical Christianity. But here too I had to point out the differences – *communio versus unio* – approach as opposed to fusion.

We worked for a long time. An 'hour' in this pastoral college always lasted seventy-five minutes. After that there was a brief pause, and then another seventy-five minutes, which often proved longer. Then came sabbath. I could not implement my cheerful proposal that we should spend it in Berlin in the Jewish community – there was not enough transport: that many people would not fit into the tiny Trabants. I was to make a sabbath for them. The table was laid as a festal table. With great difficulty they found brass lamps and a brass chalice for the wine. Two *challot* (*barches*) and cheese, butter, coffee or tea. It turned into a marvellous sabbath festival. I sang the prayers, had to explain the customs and say the grace at the end once again in German. My own feeling, that I had not celebrated or prayed properly, vanished before the insight into how important this evening meal was for the group.

In the afternoon we reflected on the texts for this sabbath. I began with the second chapter of the 'Sayings of the Fathers', curious to see they would approach these texts from their perspective. For example: 'Be heedful of the ruling power, for they bring no man nigh to them save for their own need: they seem to be friends such time as it is to their gain, but they stand not with a man in his time of stress' (Pirke Avot II.3). Silence. Then one cautiously said: 'Yes, that could refer to the health care in the Federal Republic, where in the end one feels completely abandoned by the state...'

Others shook their heads. They were well aware what this was about, and one then spoke with great insight about the situation of the rabbis in Roman times, when they had to act with great care under a violent rule. Then I spoke about the hidden midrashim of spiritual resistance in the time when people talked about 'Edom' and meant 'Rome', and also about Dienemann's book *Midrashim of Mourning*, from the 1930s, when the Jews in Germany said Rome and meant Berlin. But in Templin, in the group, people said nothing that attacked the state in which they lived. Later, in East Berlin, I spoke with a pastor outside the group who explained to me that these pastors, who exercised their pastoral care in this situation, in this state, could certainly see such texts as a rule of life, but not as a text which could be discussed in public. He told me a story about the text, something which had happened in his community.

A member of his community came to him in utter despair. His contract of employment with a business had been 'dissolved'. He was summoned by the police. They told him that he could do 'preliminary work against criminal attacks on the state' in his spare time. What did this mean? To keep his eyes and ears open, to report little things to the state, to write down the numbers of cars in front of a particular house, and so on. He could also keep an eye on his pastor. 'Am I to become an informer?' he asked. These terms were firmly rejected by him. Was he not a loyal citizen? he was asked. He went to the pastor for advice and help; he sent him to someone else so as not to make the situation worse.

Those who found themselves in such situations were often summoned as a group to report. If one had nothing to offer, one could come under suspicion oneself. So a good deal was invented. My friend indicated that in this way the sources of information themselves became unreliable, so that the system was obstructed more than if the aims were achieved.

I heard about a similar incident from a pastor in East Berlin. He had to go on an official journey to West Berlin, was permitted a car, but could not drive. He called up the church office to get a driver, but no one was prepared to drive him. After half an hour two men came to him and introduced themselves as technicians who had had enough there and wanted to go to the West. They were excellent drivers. They also said that there were certainly microphones in his house. They would gladly turn them off – they would come to some arrangement. The pastor was very friendly and invited them to lunch (jacket potatoes with butter and salt). He tried to make them respectable citizens again. Why shouldn't the state hear his conversations? There were no secrets here. And why do you want to refuse the state the fruits of your education? Stay here! They went away. 'They thought I was a fool,' he said.

On this visit the state proved well disposed to me. When the message about my visit reached Templin, a phone call from Berlin was immediately made to the Templin community: 'A rabbi is coming! What's the position over the memorial at the Jewish cemetery?' And the next day people were working there. Members of the community went voluntarily to remove the weeds. A Frau Schilz had managed to get a memorial stone erected there after long years: 'This is the last resting place of the Jewish community in Templin.' Now a bench was also put up there (chained to prevent theft). The wall was renovated and new steps were made up the hill. Everything was prepared, but people were sensitive and did not say a word to me about it. However, when I expressed a wish to visit the Jewish cemetery, there were sighs of relief.

I wanted to go up alone, but that was not possible. A whole pilgrimage group accompanied me, and some of those who had taken so much trouble over the work stood by the small hill outside the city wall. The Jewish community had already left in 1920, and there were no longer any tombstones. Only the hill and the simple monument. They asked my advice about what sort of memorial ceremony they could arrange for 9 November. Then they would also put a plate on a shed which had perhaps once been the Jewish school. So a Jewish presence lived on here – although people had hardly seen a Jew for seventy years. I am not sure what my short visit to the pastoral college was able to achieve – but the permission for a further development of the memorial area came after a two-day visit of a rabbi to Templin.

The invisible Jew in this area... A pastor told me of his church near the family castle of the Arnims, where Bettina also once lived. 'Now it's a centre for writers and artists', he said. Very near is a small Jewish cemetery, with only thirteen graves. But the artists who visit the castle always insist on visiting these tombs. If there are no Jews with whom one can speak, perhaps such a conversation is important, a memorial place where people still hear us.

Early in the morning, on the last day, I went back into the forest. I wanted to talk to comrade Lenin again. But he was not alone. There was a roe deer on the slope looking at the monument. The deer disappeared, and I sat down:

'We've been talking about the Sayings of the Fathers, Comrade Vladimir,' I told him, 'and my colleagues have some difficulties with the following passage:

> Consider three things and thou wilt not fall into the hands of transgression: know what is above thee – a seeing eye and a hearing ear and all thy deeds written in a book.

The pastors saw this as only a religious saying about the relationship of man to God and were very fatalistic. And so I told them about the ten days of repentance where the written word is sealed only on the tenth day, and where in this way you can begin a new book. I did not dare to move on to the political level. But I was inevitably remined of the great, all-seeing brother, of the state. What do you think about it?'

Ask Lenin.

But he did not want to give me any satisfaction.

'Perestroika,' I admonished him, 'Glasnost!'

Some newspapers in the small library of the pastoral college had discussed this theme, and I wanted to read Lenin a text which was devoted to his works of precisely sixty-five years previously, after his fifty-third birthday (his last). He was paralysed and could not come to the twelfth party conference. His letter to the party conference was not sent because of Stalin, nor printed. This letter to the party conference begins with the words, 'I would very much recommend that a number of changes to our political structure should be made at this party conference.'

The Rashi text on this, the exegesis by Igor Yakovlev in the *Moscow News*, stated: 'It was about the necessity and imperative need for democratization, which would guarantee a normal development of the country, a smooth transition from one period to another, and in this connection also a change of the personnel involved. All that the Soviet citizens achieved only later; it was only recognized by them after long and tragic decades' (*Moscow News*, May 1988, 3).

I was delighted to read this text. On this sabbath morning I had also had to expound the *parasha* for this week, the text *b'ha alotcha* from Leviticus, the chapter on the seventy elders who were to undertake the work with Moses, to whom a spirit of prophecy was given. Two of them, Eldad and Medad, did not come along out of modesty. But the spirit of prophecy seized them and they prophesied in the camp. 'Destroy them,' said the ambitious Joshua to Moses, because he saw them as an attack on his own position. Were things to become so democratic that anyone could prophesy? But Moses replied, 'I only wish that everyone in Israel would become a prophet!'

'Does this refer to you, Comrade Vladimir?' I asked him.

Ask...

And so I went back to the group, out of the forest.

I returned to East Berlin, in time for the service. Peter Kirchner, a surgeon and leader of the congregation, is a good friend. But this morning he was not at the service in Rykestrasse. And Isaac Neumann, who had begun as rabbi in the congregation the previous autumn, had again decided not to attend the service. We had been fellow students in Cincinnati, and I had found him a dear, honest person. But very nervous, filled with anxiety – after all, he came to us from the extermination camp, from Auschwitz. Gentle, very withdrawn, he had devoted himself to work in the American rabbinate. I was amazed that he had accepted the post in East Berlin with all its pressures. Unfortunately he failed in the task, and I wanted to talk with him. I went to his house with a friend because he was not in the synagogue, but he was not at home.

In reflecting on this sorry situation, the collapse of the

relationship between congregation and rabbi, it became clear to me that the problem was the situation, not the person. Isaac came here with a great love of people and a reformer's zeal. He wanted to show what was new in America – and he did not have the patience to do this very slowly. He succeeded in some things. When, in advance, he told the people on the eve of the sabbath what passages in the morning Torah reading would cause problems, and how they could reflect on them, his efforts at teaching pleased many. And he was also very ready to help. But his attempt to introduce new music into the service failed to recognize the feelings in the congregation, which wanted to go on using the old familiar melodies. That he wanted to shorten the service, that his sermons were perhaps longer than customary, would have been no reason for conflict had that conflict not already been there. Isaac saw his position in terms of the American model; the congregation in East Berlin had quite a different conception. Peter Kirchner wanted to help by explaining the situation to Isaac. But Isaac saw this as interference in his work and did not understand that Peter worked for the congregation, gave up his spare time and also had to attempt being an intermediary between the community and the authorities.

Isaac was afraid of the authorities: he feared that his letters could be opened and that telephone conversations could be tapped. He often went to the American embassy, safe territory, where he could read the American newspapers and feel at home. The text from Pirke Avot, 'be heedful of the ruling power', was an injunction which he did not want to obey. Unfortunately the attacks on him became personal, and referred to the pressures of the situation, to which he could not do justice. But equally it is necessary to counter his attacks on Peter Kirchner. Peter's honesty and decency were particularly important at this time, and another saying from this chapter of Pirke Avot fits that: 'And let all them that labour with the congregation labour with them for the sake of Heaven, for the merit of the fathers supports them.' If one recalls the Nachman affair, the embezzlement of many millions from the Jewish community by a leading representative, then one must especially recognize the righteousness of the two men in this conflict in the East Berlin Jewish congregation.

It is true that every rabbi is attacked; that goes with the situation and is part of his job. At the same time, in West Berlin one heard attacks on Rabbi Ernst Stein, one of my pupils at Leo Baeck College, who for years had proved himself by excellent work in the congregation. After the funeral of the well-known television star Hanns Rosenthal, disgruntled accusations were heard against the rabbi: he had held the service quite late on the Friday afternoon, had yielded to the wishes of the media, had let Rosenthal's non-Jewish son say Kaddish. I can only say that I would have acted precisely as Ernst Stein acted. I make this comparison simply to show that these gibes passed Ernst by and did not mean anything because the relationship between him and the congregation is a secure one. In the case of Isaac it was impossible for such a relationship to have developed. I am convinced that a more cautious beginning, an attempt to understand the situation of the congregation, would have been successful. Isaac Neumann and Peter Kirchner could certainly have established a partnership. But the pressure was too great, and there was not enough time. It made me sad. I had achieved something with my Christian friends. He had not found the way to his Jewish friends. Isaac returned to the USA. But there is always next time.

Three days later, in my room in Wuppertal, I heard a radio broadcast on 'Jews in the DDR'. The media had all come to Isaac Neumann's farewell service, and I even heard part of his sermon. It was a word of reconciliation.

'Not everything was good.. not everything was bad... I hope that the new rabbi will be as good as Moses, as patient and as wise as Solomon...' Peter Kirchner had an immediate answer: 'He must have humanity!' The wounds had not yet been healed.

The very fair broadcast also mentioned the other problems which had led Isaac to his decision: the anti-Zionist press, the pressure on a Jew living utterly alone. Interviews with members of the congregation brought out the same thing.

'I have to know the history of a family... now and then,

meeting Christians, I got into a situation where the host talked about his fine time as a soldier in Paris,' said one of the young people in the congregation. Others indicated that the community got 300,000 marks a year from the government and that the Jews in the DDR were valued: 'The Jews who returned to Germany, to the DDR, did so out of conviction. They were politically committed, did not want to go to the Federal Republic with Neo-Nazis... I have great confidence in Honecker because he was in the nick for ten years, in concentration camps, in Buchenwald. So it doesn't worry me if a vegetable seller on the corner is antisemitic.'

There was a long interview with Peter Kirchner's son in the broadcast. Many of his friends did not come to the farewell service, to demonstrate their dissatisfaction with Isaac. But he spoke very positively about the religious life ('no kaftan is long enough for him... Kirchner would like to go to a yeshiva,' said his friends). Gerald is a medical student. And he is a seeker.

Irene Runge said: 'We could bring 30,000 to Judaism, so many want to come over... for different reasons; out of solidarity, out of curiosity, out of honest seeking. But we keep to the Halachah, also because of the old people in our community whom that would destroy... But we have a future.'

I hope so too. They must have a future. Now the East German government said that they would also introduce reparations for Jews. There is hope and a future. I hope that the new rabbi settles into this work. And that my friends come together to build up a better world, everywhere.

The Bad Cop and the
Good Cop

John the Baptist had no head for dancing. It was missing. This giant puppet went headless down the aisles of the church, between the worshippers – a somewhat unhappy element in the staging of a Rock Mass which opened the Kirchentag in Halle, East Germany. Paul Oestreicher had travelled with me from East Berlin, where he had also taken part in a large peace conference. I came from my teaching activity in the Federal Republic, and at last we had time to talk and get back to work together, though only during the car journey. In Halle we went to different working groups, although he was also in the church for the opening service. I squeezed myself on to a side bench in the church, saw too little, heard too much.

Why didn't I like it? This 'wilderness experience', in the Market Church, came to the community as the enthusiastic work of a pastor who had devoted himself entirely to the 'others', the young, the dissatisfied, rock fans, skinheads, all those who did not feel at home in the church and religion. He went away from the main church into a small community where he could work with these groups. He really wanted to arrange an 'alternative Kirchentag', but as things are – in the DDR and everywhere else – he had to fit into the system. The arrangements in his community were not in the programme for the Kirchentag proper, i.e. not approved by the authorities. So he had to have the bishop as a 'patron' – and that was an alternative! This rock mass was his contribution to the Kirchentag: moments of reflection, quiet organ music, and then the loud, stormy music, the accusations and the way into mystical, beautiful (?) thoughts.

I could forgive him the music, above all when I saw the

young people and the body movements which stressed their involvement in the event. But not the ideas. These demonstrated that he had learned too little – from his teachers, from history, from his religion and from his fellow human beings. So a latent, unconscious antisemitism arose in these mystical texts, which represented a kind of undigested thought of Khalil Gibran. The temple curtain with the menorah again tore from top to bottom, Christ triumphed, the Jews lost and the community attached itself to the dancing John to go into the wilderness (the 'wilderness' was the destroyed St George's Church which is now being rebuilt). Really a beautiful idea – but did this pastor know who John the Baptist was? What he taught? What significance conversion and repentance had in his time? Perhaps it was over-bold to believe that I as a rabbi could tell him anything about this – but in that case they should not have invited me to this Kirchentag in the DDR.

I had some anxieties from the beginning. Skinheads with Hitler salutes and Fascist ideas had been condemned at a court shortly before the Kirchentag in Halle, and a local newspaper reported that pupils in Halle took the skinheads of East Berlin as a model. In their school, as in all schools in the DDR, the Hitler period was throughly discussed, and most pupils visited a former concentration camp. Nevertheless Fascist symbolism was spreading through the country. East German commentators and judges asserted that the Western media had to bear responsibility for these ideas having been smuggled into East Germany. But Peter Kirchner, the president of the Jewish congregation in East Berlin, warned that the increase of skinheads could not simply be attributed to the Western media. Brawling skinheads, their clothing, their remarks and ideas, were also a product of East German popular education. When it is remembered that one really sees very little antisemitism in the DDR, these new phenomena are particularly threatening. At a time when the anti-Israeli views are somewhat more muted, this is a particular cause for anxiety.

Disturbances were expected in Halle, since there would be protests 'from below', which would disrupt the Kirchentag. But that did not happen. Late in the evening of the first day I went with many other people through the streets to the market place. Black leather jackets, small unruly groups were there – but nothing special. However, there was not the mood, the joy, the religious feeling on this night that I had often felt at Kirchentage. There were only a few thousand, not 100,000 as in the West. And it was the first day.

The slogan of the Kirchentag was 'Repentance takes us further', and in our working group in the Petruskirche this was extended: 'Repentance takes us further – in understanding between Jews and Christians.' The group which had decided to sign on for this working group was the largest, and the church was full to bursting. Song, devout silence and a great readiness to be taught characterized this group, though I found less readiness for open criticism. Was this also a result of training in school? The first report was a thoroughly academic study of the main theme, 'The Christian and his Jewish Brothers'. Then followed Ernst Stein with 'The Jew and his Christian Brothers' – and the group woke up.

Ernst did not give an academic report. He spoke as rabbi of the West Berlin congregation. A colleague and former student of mine, he had changed in these eight years. As he said to me before his address, he had become harder. He had taken 700 funerals in these eight years. The congregation still existed and in recent times had even grown larger, partly through emigrants from the USSR. But Ernst Stein saw Judaism and the Jews in Germany as a terminal phenomenon. Perhaps this was also evident in his encounter with Isaac Neumann, who had appeared in East Berlin with great hopes and many misunderstandings: he wanted to open a bowling alley in the synagogue to bring in the youth. What youth? Ernst Stein had asked him. Isaac's congregation, which needed him most, was in old people's homes, which he seldom visited. So, as I have already said, Isaac went back to America. Ernst Stein still visited East Berlin and looked after the Jews; they were his task. And Ernst was ready to talk with Christians – but not simply to get over the past in a gracious way. He spoke sharply and clearly, remembered what had happened, and also pointed out the contrast betwen Christians and Jews: 'Christianity needs Judaism and Christians need Jews. But Jews do not need Christians.'

The audience was shattered. Many were simple, honest

Christians, who felt called to proclaim the saviour, and they wanted to take this testimony to the Jews, but stood in a history which posed obstacles here. Others were aware that the roots of Christianity lie in the Hebrew text. They knew that the first statement by Rabbi Stein was the simple truth. But the second! Did not Christianity mean more in the world? And so we arrived at the platform discussion. I sat next to Ernst, and the questions never stopped. At the cinema, thrillers often depict the police during interrogation (as a child in Germany I too had had this experience), and there are a 'bad' cop and a 'good' cop who interrogate the criminals. One is sharp and aggressive and sees the suspect only in the worst light. He is out for confessions. His partner is completely on his side. He too wants to make the the person under interrogation confess, but through kind, reassuring words. That was my role. The 'good' cop and the 'bad' interrogator. Ernst had further duties, I remained. I understood his attack. The fact that he had disturbed people showed that he was on the right track. I had to support his work, but also to show that this solved only part of the problem. The Christian reports clearly showed that those who gave them were aware of their Jewish roots, that they too knew the development in Judaism from the biblical writings through the oral Torah, the rabbinic commentaries on the Talmud and later times. This development did not really need Christianity, as Ernst said. But did Jews need Christians?

'We need our fellow human beings,' I said, and spoke of the particularity which must be realized universally, of the *mitzvot*, the religious duties, which represent the way to the other person. The Christian as a fellow human being is indispensable to us, and we do not want the Christian as an opponent. Here I was not speaking as the good cop seeking to entice the other to confessions. I had to speak as a pastor, had to encounter them on their level. But it was Ernst who so shook them that they were aroused from their convenient confidence. The 'bad' cop brought a bitter but healing medicine. His partner had to help them along the way to self-knowlege.

The partnership extended beyond the Kirchentag. I gave a lecture on the sabbath in which I had to demonstrate the historical and religious dimensions, which would do justice to the mystical and the messianic elements and could bring together the laws and customs. Ernst gave an introduction to the service on the Friday evening, and then we went to the synagogue, to lead this service. It was and had to be Ernst's service – he was the rabbi who would come when one of the four members of the congregation died. Four members! But more than a hundred were at the service in the synagogue, which had once been a house of prayer at the cemetery. I stood alongside Ernst and read some of the prayers (the congregation even had some valuable books, but no sabbath prayer book. So I took a Pesach book, which contained the evening service). Ernst's sermon was addressed to the congregation, supplemented by visitors from Magdeburg and Leipzig. Cantors came from Leipzig and from the Kirchentag, and one of them nobly held back to let his colleague sing. In the sermon Ernst again showed his pessimism, but there was also a positive element.

The next day I spoke on Mark 1.1-17. Why did they need a rabbi to investigate a New Testament text? But someone in the preparatory group had thought it would be a good idea to have the rabbi expound the New Testament and a Christian scholar a Hebrew text. I was not so enthusiastic. But it gave me an opportunity to demonstrate some of the Jewish elements in the gospel. And there we returned to the theatrical opening ceremony. Who and what was John the Baptist? I said first of all that I had got to know John the Baptist in the wilderness – only the wilderness was in Tunisia and the Baptist was the British film star Michael York. I described something of the film work with Zeffirelli and the six- hour film *Jesus of Nazareth*, where I had been introduced to the conflicts in the popular interpretation of Jesus. In this way I came to my real theme.

Behind John the Baptist stands the wilderness – not just a place of destruction, which is how it is usually seen, a devilish domain, failure, but the wilderness as a place of revelation, of encounter with the word of God in the burning bush, on Sinai, in the cave after the storm. The wilderness in the Bible is the land where one can rediscover oneself, become detached from materialism as John does; a part of creation which is not only a refuge but the land of renewal. The wilderness is the framework for the life of the prophets. Here Moses proves himself. Hither Elijah and Amos come. Hosea and Jeremiah describe the wilderness as youth, as the place of the covenant which constantly renews itself. And the wilderness belongs to everyone: as the rabbis say, the Torah was given in the wilderness, to open it up to all humankind.

John cannot be understood without this wilderness dimension. His teachings are prophetic teachings, in the tradition of Amos and Elijah. John speaks of repentance, of conversion – the Hebrew word *teshuva* means both, and both are required. Did 'the whole country of Judah' go to him in the wilderness? And what was his baptism? The Hebrew intransitive verb signifies that one baptizes oneself, is prompted by this to take one's own steps towards repentance, the recognition of sins, conversion. The later Pauline saying about the one who is to come, who baptizes with the Spirit, is a further Christian development which one has to recognize, but I had to point out that it came later. And yet, at this Kirchentag in Halle, I could show how ways can come together again: Bonhoeffer's teaching on discipleship, on the penultimate and the last things, this conversion and work for the poor, the suffering – this ethical action can be found in Judaism and in Christian teaching. Bonhoeffer's saying about cheap grace also bears witness to the importance of action before the last time. With Kafka, I then said somewhat sorrowfully: 'The messiah does not come on the last day, but on the day after.' But the problem of discipleship is shared work between Jews and Christians, and makes Christians realize that John the Baptist was a Jewish figure who bears witness for his own people and has made the Jews indispensable for Christianity. So Bonhoeffer also wrote, 'The Jew keeps the question of Christ open,' to continue the link with the Jewish people in authentic, incessant encounter. Jesus is and remains a Jewish figure.

It was difficult for these believing Christians, even in the year 1988, in the time after Auschwitz, to accept this and to allow the Jews a place alongside them. The doctrine of disinheritance remained as poison in the air. 'But Jesus says, "I am the way"' – can't you accept that?' a nice girl asked me. 'Jesus spoke from his tradition,' I said. 'The way, that is the Torah, the Halachah, the lifelong task of the Jews, the commandments, the least of which he did not want to remove – can you accept that?' 'How far do you believe in the teaching of Jesus? In his resurrection? In him as Son of God?', was the next question. With great patience I described the teaching of Jesus, how it related to the Pharisaic system (later misinterpreted by Christians), and how it developed out of this Jewish teaching.

'The silence of the rabbi on the other questions is also an answer,' the chairman then said. Some nodded. 'No, I don't understand,' came the comment from the audience, 'does he believe in the resurrection or not? I want to have a yes or a no,' said an angry older man. 'Very well then, no!' I said – the good cop is not always polite.

Further questions, but also anxious gestures from the organizers – I had to leave the platform, the Oberbürgermeister was waiting for the foreign ecumenical guests. I had to go to the reception, although these questions were much more important. When I appeared, no one noticed me. Paul in his black clothes, with the beautiful Coventry cross, was the focal point for the photographers. I put on my black kippah. The lenses shifted: the rabbi was there. Then came the obligatory picture: Oberbürgermeister, Rumanian bishop, Canon Oestreicher, Rabbi Friedlander. Only Comrade Honecker was absent: but his picture was certainly on the same page in *Neues Deutschland*.

Dialogue in the DDR.

The Rumanian bishop represented the great group of German Christians in Rumania with its own congregations and schools. He wanted to show me how Jews had at least been partially protected by Rumanians: they went to labour camps, but not to the extermination camps of their German allies. He quoted the Jews of Czernowitz, and also Paul Celan, who preferred to be in Rumania when the Red Army came. And he spoke with great respect of Chief Rabbi Rosen in Rumania. That he also continually addressed me as Chief Rabbi was the fault of the Kirchentag: my name was billed in this way everywhere, and I could only inwardly ask Lord Jakobovits for forgiveness – he is the only one called 'Chief Rabbi' in England.

So much else happened in those days. At Kirchentage I always learn, but I learned in a quite special way in the DDR. The closed nature of a society where there are some freedom zones can also lead to greater openness at other points. I wanted to remain longer, and was also to have given a dialogue sermon, but there were other dates to keep. The group recognized my obligations when it saw the American diplomatic car outside the church waiting for me. What they could not know was that it was the long arm from Wilkes Barre, Pennsylvania, which was again stretching out for me. My Bar Mitzvah pupil from the American embassy had arranged an urgent appointment for the evening – the final game between the Soviet Union and Holland, recorded that afternoon on cassette – and Jonathan Greenwald and Gaby simply took me away so that I could visit them in East Berlin. The journey led through Grünau, but I could not find the Undine Rowing Club where so much of my youth had been spent. The past is a distant land that one cannot always reach. The neighbourhood was beautiful; an evening in the Trout Quintet Restaurant, then football and much thoughtful conversation. The next day we went to Tegel airport, passing by a disputed area of Berlin which was partly occupied by demonstrators. And then I was back in Wuppertal, to continue my visiting lectureship at the Kirchliche Hochschule, along with Bertold Klappert. But he is so good and decent that I immediately decided this time to be the 'bad' cop.

Jacqueline du Pré and Dorothee Sölle

The hardest thing in the life of a rabbi is the daily encounter with death. In Judaism we know death as part of life: is not the cemetery called the 'house of life'? At the beginning of daily morning prayer we thank God who 'has breathed a pure soul into us... which he will take from us one day, to give it back at the end of time'. A profound book of Jewish thought of our time is Franz Rosenzweig's *The Star of Redemption*, in which death is recognized as the crown of creation (Genesis 1, 'And behold, it was very (*m'od*) good; *v'hineh tov m'od* has the interpretation *tov ha-movet*, 'death is good'). But at a time of death we do not shut ouselves up in mourning. We live in this world, not in the next, and we are aware of the loss.

Israel Bettan, my professor of homiletics in Cincinnati, taught us about sermons at funerals. Look down, then around, and then up. First talk about the dead person, then about the family in their mourning, and then at the end give comfort and hope for the future (he left it open whether he meant 'heaven').

Nevertheless it remains difficult. Most rabbis have been 'married' for many years to a congregation; they know every member, and their own grief and loss shows itself at every funeral. A child... a worthy old lady who embodied compassion and decency in a special way... someone who survived Auschwitz... each death deprives us of part of our existence. Once, when I was a university rabbi in New York, I went to the conveyor belt at Riverside Chapel, where there is a funeral every twenty minutes. The rabbis there were exploited as cannon fodder; I didn't know what my one piece of help amounted to. It was terrible. I was allowed hardly any time to talk to the family, nor did they expect that. The people appeared ten minutes before the service and above all wanted to greet their friends. Never again! The function of a priest in his ministry can perhaps protect him – rabbis are not used to that sort of thing.

I was one of the mourners at the burial of Jacqueline du Pré, the great cellist, and I also had to give the funeral address. I just wanted to weep, but the television lights were glaring in my face, so I had to escape into the sermon (the broadcast transmission was then so abbreviated that it communicated only the hope and not the sorrow of my talk). Daniel Barenboim, Itzhak Perlman, Zubin Mehta, Rostropovich and others accompanied the coffin from the house of prayer to the grace, where a colleague spoke the closing prayers. There I could weep and give expression to my sorrow; I had lost so much with her.

In the six years before her death I had visited her almost every week. Saturday afternoon, around 5.30, was a firm date for both of us. But that did not mean that we only saw each other then. From time to time the telephone would ring – 'I'm so lonely, do come over' – and I came. She lived nearby in London, in Rutland Gardens, three houses away from my home and synagogue. Margot Fonteyn had let her have the house, a lovely home which she had built for her paralysed husband Arias, with wheelchair ramps and a lift. In these rooms, which combined elegance and warmth, Jacqueline was as happy as she could be. On a few occasions she came to service in the synagogue in her wheelchair and then came up to have lunch with us afterwards. But that happened only rarely; usually I went to her. When other duties made Saturday impossible, we looked for another time.

Then Jacqueline had to move, to a beautiful apartment in Notting Hill Gate, which had previously been a convent school. It was only fifteen minutes by bus, and our arrangement became all the firmer; it had become important for both of us.

A good deal has been written about Jacqueline du Pré. Some of it is myth, some of it is attacks on the family, some of it is true. But the real truth cannot be found in the texts, but lives on in the music – the song does not cease with the singer – and in the memories which constantly bring us back to the blessing and the tragedy of her life. These memories become small and pale if we try to put them into words.

In Judaism there is no confession and no secret of the confessional. There is more: understanding of the private realm and the structure of the encounter in conversation which belongs to two people and is not to be passed on. Ruth Ann, Jacqueline's faithful nurse, friend and guardian, always shut the door when I came. However, it can be said that she took part nevertheless, since she was indeed Jacqueline's *alter ego*. One cannot say anything about this time without mentioning Ruth Ann. She is 'one of the righteous' of this world, someone who voluntarily gave up her own life and personal development for twelve years to look after Jacqueline. As a convinced Christian she went to a prayer meeting every day, sang in the choir, prayed for Jacqueline and brought her faith to her. Perhaps she saw me as the representative of the 'other' religion, but we understood and respected each other. Sometimes in the mists of her illness Jacqueline saw Ruth Ann as the 'warder' of her fearful prison, and I had to make a joke. Then she again remembered the love and goodness which came to her through Ruth Ann; understanding of the illness surrounded her in dark times.

A Hasidic story tells of a father and child in a dark wood. 'What do we do if we are separated?' asks the child. 'In that case you must call, and I will call, if we are wandering around in the dark wood. As long as we don't stop calling we will find one another,' the father replied. Jacqueline and I had found each other in this dark wood. We sat together and told each other stories. As another Hasidic story goes, we had found fire in a particular place in the wood from which healing could come. But it did not come. However, I listened, hours and weeks and months and years. The stories did not change with the increasing pressure of the illness. Most of those who now want to write about Jacqueline know her only from this late period and therefore have the wrong idea of her. I cannot reply to them; what is private remains private. However, I have to point out that the only ones who may write about Jacqueline's life are those who went with her all the way. But does one have to reply at all?

Memories of the good times were woven into the dark picture that could not be pushed to one side. For many, for her friends and for the world, she was 'Smiley', the one who was always laughing, whose *joie de vivre* always had to be visible. That was not necessary between us, although the *joie de vivre* was always there. Now and then she would say even to me – and not only to me: 'For God's sake, tell me another sad story. My problem is that I can't cry.' And she couldn't.

I brought friends to her: poets, who read her their poems but were forced to see how her concentration went after a few minutes; Donald Swann came and played and sang his songs, of which she was very fond. She wanted to include his 'Hippopotamus Song' or the 'London Bus' in her 'Desert Island Discs' radio broadcast, but there was already too much material and the broadcast could not be extended. Sometimes I read some psalms with her, but she was not particularly interested in them.

We occasionally talked about religion, but it was rarely the main topic of our conversation. Jacqueline du Pré was a Jew, but she had become a Jew too quickly and too easily. Daniel Barenboim and Jacqueline came to Israel in the Six Day War to play for the troops. They were full of enthusiasm. They wanted to get married and Jacqueline was converted to Judaism – in a day! That's what she wanted. That's what Ben Gurion wanted. Usually it takes years of study to become a Jew – but the rabbinate in Israel is a law to itself. One day, including immersion and an examination before the rabbinic court. Now they wanted to get married. As the story goes, the rabbis were flabbergasted: 'But one has to wait months after baptism,' they said, 'it would be a sin.' But clever Daniel, with his knowledge of the Talmud, is said to have remarked: 'Which is the greater sin, to get married straight away or to live together straight away?' So they got married.

Jacqueline did not enter into a covenant of faith, but a covenant with Daniel, with Aida (her good mother-in-law whom she loved ardently), with Pinchas, Itzhak and all Israel. This covenant also counts. When we talked about it she was well enough aware of that. She was no longer a Christian, much to the grief of her pious family. She was a Jew, but one of those who confront God in doubt and hesitation, yet nevertheless identify with the Jewish family, though they themselves do not have much to do with religion.

'I hate fanaticism in all religions', she often said to me. She always remained free, but the freedom never alienated her from Judaism. In her Jewish family, in Israel, she saw Judaism as part of a special, private existence. The Israeli virtuosos who surrounded the two of them had made themselves a very private world, perhaps the only world in which Daniel feels free and at home. But this group also travelled all over the world, and so took its private Jewish life with it. The difference between Jacqueline and her Christian family caused them both grief. Jacqueline could nevertheless recognize that the steadfastness of her mother in her last illness was based on faith in Jesus and helped to soothe the suffering. Jacqueline's way was a different one, certainly harder, the way of a special freedom.

Music was a religion which brought instruction, called for sacrifice, gave much and never abandoned her. When talk became more difficult, we listened to her records: '...at least I recorded everything I wanted to,' she would often say. We also talked about other things which had influenced her, books which to begin with she could still read, before memory and sight began to fail. Fritz Perl's therapy interested her, although she learned far more from her own therapist. Sometimes she talked about the Holocaust, partly because this came to her through many of her friends. She always shuddered, but did not want to change the subject. A woman friend who visited her weekly had the Auschwitz number tattooed on her wrist; others had escaped at the last moment, had somehow survived. Sometimes when we talked about it I was reminded of Sylvia Plath, but in Jacqueline's case this was no pathological attraction to the deepest suffering, but the rejection of the roughness and hatred that she saw in the world.

Most of her visitors were Jewish, but every name in her diary was something special. Finally it became almost a ritual to take this book and read the names from the previous week and the week to come. In this way one could enjoy past hours again and create expectations for the future. And in times of great loneliness she could convince herself that she was not forgotten. It became a game: 'What does this mean, Stephen B-K?', I would ask, and she replied with a laugh, 'Bishop Kovacevich'. He, too, was really loyal in his visits. William Wordsworth was a direct descendant of the poet, and also compiled a small book about her. Lady Barbirolli came often, Anna Helb always, and also many whose visits were more difficult. The entries in the book ranged from aristocrats to the fireman and the chauffeur (they were collecting money for multiple sclerosis and Jacqueline wanted to encourage them). Members of my congregation came to take her to a restaurant or a concert. And the cellists! Jacqueline was friendly and ready to help, but these visits weren't always a delight. In the last three months I once brought a mother with a gifted child, but I saw how difficult such visits were. Her old friends came, Rodney Friend and William Pleeth, and others – but never enough. More and more pages in the diary would remain empty, and then Ruth Ann would telephone people and build ways through the wilderness. There were also glorious days when Jacqueline could tell me of a call or a letter from Prince Charles. And slowly, slowly, she went deeper into the dark valley of suffering.

So many memories...

The last days. On the evening of Kol Nidre I came with her tape of the Kol Nidre melody and found that Ruth Ann had already put the record on. Jacqueline and I listened to it, and I talked with her about Yom Kippur, the Day of Atonement. A few weeks later I described this in one of my broadcasts on the BBC World Service – Jacqueline's family and friends in Israel heard it two days before the news of her death.

On the last day of her life I came and found many friends in the room. Ruth Ann took me into the bedroom and put on the Kol Nidre melody again. She left us and we were alone for the last time. Jacqueline had not been able to speak for several days, but it was still possible to read something in her eyes. So I looked at her, held her hand in mine, and recited the last prayers of the Jewish tradition for this moment. It was difficult to be a rabbi, and even more difficult to say goodbye as a friend. But we all knew that death was now coming to her as a friend, after long suffering. She was ready, even if we were not. I sat there for a while, sunk in thought. Then I kissed her and went home. she died three hours later. I believe that the last person to hold her hand was the Duchess of Kent.

Every rabbi has an unforgettable memory of a funeral. The memory speaks to him of an abiding blessing, and also of a grief which attaches itself to his family loss. The closing word in the Jewish eulogy is always the same: *'y'hi zecher zaddik l'v'racha* – the memory of the just remains as a blessing.' In our recollection we kept coming back to the suffering of this courageous, great, laughing, suffering girl, who never grew old. Nor will the memory grow old.

The music plays on. In the world, in my life.

I sent these pages about one remarkable woman to another remarkable woman, Dorothee Sölle. I wrote to her:

Dear Dorothy,

How can something like this really come about?

Perhaps only through love, through the dialogue that brings us together, through the hopes that bear us up.

I heard later that Fulbert had knocked on the door of the great church in Frankfurt where I gave my opening sermon for the Kirchentag. The door did not open. And I think of the many times when we were prevented from meeting – but what does that mean compared with reality? Cologne, New York, London – everywhere in the world, and now in a book.

In Hanover I wanted to hear poems, but the line of people waiting extended over three streets. Then I went to the window and introduced myself: 'I am the translator of Erich Fried and Dorothee Sölle, from London'. Something strange happened: the truth was rewarded with success. So we sat together at the window, talked about poems, listened to the loving-hating Erich and learned from him and from one another.

At that time in Hanover I could not go to the Feminist Conference, to the 'Women of Nineveh'. But shortly before-hand I met old Ben Amittai, running desperately through the streets, with wild, dishevelled hair.

'Where are you going, Jonah?' I shouted to him.

'Leave me be, no one understands me,' he lamented.

'With your old-fashioned Hebrew...', I began, not wanting to criticize him and his book. I also knew (through Kreuz Verlag) that the women had said many profound things about the text. I indicated this.

'No one understands it,' he muttered. 'Never mind. I've struggled with God. And I was right. No one now remembers the abomination that was done by them then. Did God have to give a Persil coupon, a letter of absolution, after forty days?'

'But it's a question of God's forgiveness,' I said cautiously.

'You too?', he said in amazement, 'I'm already frowned on – the old avenging Jew, from the line of patriarchs, who understands nothing of love. My old father is said to have drummed Prussian loyalty into me, though my mother...' He stopped and reflected.

'What those people said about my mother was very interesting,' he conceded. 'And I liked the justified attacks on idiotic sermons. What are the men thinking about, who identify themselves so much with their problems and with me? The women understood more, even about the situation in Nineveh. Since then I've thought far more about the women of Nineveh. But still, they didn't understand me.'

'How and why?' I asked.

'Wrong glasses,' he said quite simply. 'Even the contact lenses didn't fit. Sometimes I really despair. I would give up completely, but then people come along like that Dorothee Sölle and that Elisabeth Moltmann and Luise Schottroff, to fight against antisemitism in feminist theology. Have you read the book? (I nodded) Good. Justified accusations against the writing of the fathers lead to new insights – but the Torah and Hebrew scripture have far more to say. Historically-conditioned mistakes should not distract us from the teaching. And the other "glasses"' – he looked round to see whether anyone was eavesdropping on us – 'the other "glasses" are Christianity. They still read this text as a less valuable preface to the New Testament. That the people of Nineveh suddenly believed in God and began to go on the way of repentance is seen as "part of the theology of the cross". And then they say of me, "he cannot immerse himself in the unconditional love of God, so that makes him forget to ask, 'And where am I?'" Where were they when I jumped into the water? That was a "leap of faith"!'

'That Elizabeth was talking about the same thing,' I ventured to say. 'It's all the same,' he insisted. '*Ivri anochi* – I'm a Hebrew! That was utter trust in God, which never left me. When she quoted Klaus Heinrich, "For Jonah the gracious and merciful God is a wavering God, unreliable and unfaithful," I saw red. That I could not understand God was a daily event; that I attacked him for his decision to save Nineveh was a question to him which I do not change.'

I did not completely believe him. He was too hurt by the failure of his prophecy. But I knew that he was sure in his trust in God. And Annemarie had taken his side. He recognized that.

'Great,' he said, 'I can understand myself better through the women of Nineveh. If they don't want to say good-bye to me – "because we are Jonah, because we are part of Nineveh, because Jonah is part of Nineveh, because God loves Jonah and Nineveh", I'm quite satisfied.'

'You haven't finished the quotation,' I warned him. 'She also says, "The story of Nineveh can become reality if we are not converted to God, to ourselves and to others."'

'That's true,' he said with great sorrow, 'they didn't understand me. It was not a fairy tale. It was history. Elisabeth was right when she said that the text is eschatologically open. But the history was closed. *Nineveh was destroyed*. That great city, with its heroes, where no sisterhood could develop, existed for only seventy years and disappeared from the world. Grace was accepted as a well-deserved present, and people quickly lapsed into their old ways. Perhaps...,' he looked at me hopefully, 'perhaps this time things will be different. The Shekhinah entered into the suffering world. One day it must succeed. Do you still think that I'm waiting only for destruction? I'm waiting for repentance, for a new love and righteousness under the dust of repentance.'

'Where have you been all this time?' I asked with some curiosity.

'I stayed in Nineveh and preached righteousness, but no one understood me,' said the son of Amittai, parting company from me and becoming a shadow in the night.

You must understand, Dorothee, that this review stems from a recognition of the sisterhood. I am well aware that the tiny mistakes of the sisters are not on the same level as the great mistakes of the brothers. Something new is happening in the world. Jonah is beginning to hope. And now I'm sending you a little story about Jacqueline, which is also a big story about Ruth Ann and a great loyalty, so that you too can have hope for the future.

With love,

Albert

France and Elie Wiesel

You can't hate France.

Paris is the most beautiul city in the world, especially in spring and late autumn, a time when the tourists have gone and the Parisians are back again. Friends of France have to be there, because then you fall in love with France all over again.

This sense of being in love does not last very long for me. Fear returns; perhaps it's always been there in the background. The only way of staying in love a bit is not to surrender completely, to play a role which makes it possible to confine a love affair to a particular time: one comes and remains as a tourist. Evelyn and I have the most marvellous memories of the places where we have stayed on holiday: Perpignan, Canet Plage, Ceret, Albi, St Paul de Vence – golden times. Evelyn also knows how to go on holiday properly. We were once travelling through the Loire area and I found an attractive, simple, cheap hotel. She did not say 'no' directly, but in the evening we were sitting in the Château d'Artigny – three days of utter luxury and a week less holiday. She was right. And Paris remains Paris.

I feel uncomfortable and awkward in France as a Jew. Other rabbis would dispute that. Remarkably enough, many recollections return to me in the persons of rabbis. So a few years ago I was sitting in a small cafe on a Paris boulevard with Rabbi Lionel Blue at a table with bread, cheese, salad and a bottle of wine. Lionel beamed: 'Paris is so beautiful, so perfect.'

Lionel is a traveller who fits into any situation, a gourmet who can weigh up French menus and whose geniality attracts everyone. We were talking about the people going past our table, and sometimes nodding at other members of the confer-

ence looking at us enviously as they went their way to extremely
important discussions. And we knew that life was smiling on
us. At such moments I think of the great blessings of a culture
and a humanity which has given the world so much. Freedom,
style, *joie de vivre* are all French!

A few months ago I was back in Paris, staying in the home
of my friends Michael and Isabelle Williams. Michael is rabbi
of the congregation in the rue Copernic. We visited members
of the congregation, took part in a golden wedding, walked
through the streets, and loved Paris.

Then – and the world has not yet forgotten this – a bomb
exploded at the door of the synagogue, parts of which were
destroyed. People died ... 'only Jews, no French', said a
minister on the radio. Michael's criticism of the country in
which he lived was unpopular. 'You're the rabbi I heard on
television,' a taxi driver told him. 'Get out. I'm not driving
you.'

The bomb had destroyed many windows in the street. No
one was surprised when the neighbours sent the bills for repair
to the synagogue. That too is Paris, a Paris which I got to know
very well as a zealous reader of Heine's 'Paris Letters': after a
century much remains the same. Evelyn used to go with me to
Heine's grave in Montmartre and put a stone on the tomb.
Now she lets me go by myself. Paris remains a good, beautiful,
temperamental city, where many people are still convinced
that Dreyfus was a traitor. Paris.

And not just Paris. Rabbi Dow Marmur and I travelled
to Strasbourg to found a new Reform congregation there.
Sometimes I have sympathy with Christian pastors, the representatives of a church which they also have to support as
an institution, in which they have to do 'official' work. For us
it is easier. But there are sometimes moments when one
becomes a 'representative' of the institution. Dow and I now
had this honour. We were escorted from our hotel by a member
of the board of the congregation and taken to the group in a
splendid building. We spoke for hours and in the end convinced ourselves that the congregation did not want a rabbi,
as we had thought. A teacher for the school, fine. But he had
to be cheap. It began to get dark. Our host got up in some

agitation. 'We must get in the car and take you back to the hotel. Do you have plans for supper? No? I can recommend the hotel – excellent menu.'

Two hours later they picked us up again, since the group's evening programme included a dialogue report on Reform Judaism. But Strasbourg is a beautiful city, almost as beautiful as Paris.

Years later, when our World Union again met in Paris, I still hoped that something could develop in Strasbourg. So I suggested that our rabbis in Germany, perhaps Peter Levinson, could visit Strasbourg and support Reform efforts. There had to be some movement in the group somehow.

The French delegation went rigid. Then someone sprang up. 'Strasbourg will remain French!' he shouted at me.

Since Napoleon's time the Jews of France have been more French than the French. Only now, in a situation in which the Sephardic Jews from Algeria, Morocco and Tunisia have achieved a new majority, is anything changing. A new vitality has developed in the congregations. But the great history of Jews in France must not be forgotten. I once travelled with rabbi John Rayner to Geneva (John, at the wheel, always reminds me how our families came through the mountains to Andorra, in his car. He suddenly turned round to me and said in quiet amazement, 'The brakes aren't working.' John is always right, and the next half hour was very stimulating.) On the way to Geneva there were no surprises. John was happy, breathed in the air with great satisfaction, and said, 'Here we really are in Rashi's world.'

The thought of the great eleventh-century rabbi and biblical commentator and of his sons-in-law, the Tosaphists, was far from my mind as I watched a red sports car trying to overtake us. But I understood John's feeling for this landscape and for a France which is so rich in history. However, I was preoccupied more with its tragic aspects.

Once, on the way to Carcassonne our car broke down. The mechanic who looked at it couldn't suppress a chuckle when he saw the price of his summer holidays beckoning in our vehicle. But he firmly promised that it would rise again in three days and took us to a hotel in Albi. Albi, a roseate city of persecution and martyrdom. The Albigensian past came so vividly to mind that I was not sorry to leave the beautiful city after three days. There is something brutal about this country, an untamed power. It does not always break out. But the dark side appears in the most brilliant figures – for example in the antisemitism of Voltaire. The Vichy government and the leadership of the Jews in France is part of this history, and the rise of LePen in the last elections cannot be overlooked. There is something similar about the nationalistic France which made the nobility and the church join forces against Dreyfus, even if it is far removed from this past. But one must be disturbed about Archbishop Lefebvre, especially when one remembers that his supporters and those of LePen share the same ideas. LePen wants to rescue 'Christian civilization' and puts his group under the banner of Joan of Arc. Services at his gatherings are led by priests who are followers of Lefebvre. And the archbishop attacks the Second Vatican Council precisely at the point at which it spoke on the relationship between Christianity and other religions – 'satanically', as Lefebvre thinks.

Is there truth in other religions? Do Jews also love God? In that case, say the priests around Lefebvre, the church was wrong in its persecution and burning of Jews and non-Christians over the last 1600 years. If the church were wrong here, it would be possible for there to be other errors in Catholicism, even the notion that the pope is always right. So, they say, the pope must now declare that the Second Vatican Council was wrong. The archbishop was staggered that the pope had met with non-Catholics in Assisi in 1986. He has already described Paul VI and John-Paul II as 'almost heretics'. A schism in France is not only possible, but probable. Lefebvre and Le Pen and the groups around them, dogged by deep anxiety about 'the other' and intolerance, could become the foundation of a wider movement which also shows a part of French history which is now emerging again. The great ideas of revolution, love of humanity and brotherhood are in danger here. This side of French history is expressed in the great films of the post-war period, *Le chagrin et la pièté* and *Shoah*. But we must also remember the great village in which the Jews where saved by the whole community, where goodness and greatness merged in the French character: Le Chambon...

When my friend Michael Goulston, a rabbi who died prematurely, was editing our journal *European Judaism*, we arranged a dialogue with French Jews in Paris. Michael found a Balkan restaurant in Montmartre and we insisted that lots of wine should be served. The microphone was put between the wine bottles and in the end it was hardly noticed, so a lively disucssion developed: those involved included Albert Memmi, Georges Levittes (from the Jewish World Congress), Immanuel Levinas and Alan Montefiore. The evening was very lively, with disputed questions like Memmi's 'Judaicity' against the gentle, deep religious understanding of the philosopher Levinas. Two or three times *European Judaism* arranged such a dialogue, which was always instructive and ultimately hopeful.

My visit to Rabbi Michael Williams and Isabelle was in December 1987. I have to confess that I shall also regard this visit as one of the great moments of my life. Not just because friendship is so important for me. But I was in Paris because in an unguarded moment Elie Wiesel had said to me, 'Come to Paris. I've invited seventy-six Nobel Prize winners to discuss the great problems of the world. Some experts, friends and members of my new foundation for human questions will also come. So you're invited.'

Michael's apartment is only a few minutes from the Hotel Concorde, where the prize winners were staying. I went to the registration desk and introduced myself. It was a rather uncomfortable process. 'Mitterand's friends have taken over the organization,' said the American girl there, 'and now we have so many French guests that there's no room. Do you have a letter from Wiesel with you? No? Sorry, nothing doing.'

I was told that Wiesel was at the great reception in the American Embassy. But how to get there? Only with an invitation. However, *he* had that; he was going to give it to me. However, without an invitation I couldn't get to him.

I looked round, saw a Nobel Prize winner with his badge on his lapel and told him that we had to go to the Embassy. He had almost forgotten. We went in the taxi to the Embassy. The man in front of me had forgotten his invitation. 'Nothing doing,' said the policeman. 'Strict security. You've time to go back and get it.' I was next, and innocently showed him my passport. Then he asked me for the invitation. 'Professor Brown behind me has it,' I said, and went quickly into the Embassy. The man had a problem: should he run after me and leave his post? So he turned to Professor Brown, who convinced him that I was part of the group. I was in.

A nun introduced the guests to the American ambassador. I kissed her straightaway. 'Carol, it's me, Albert.' Dr Carol Rittner had run a conference in Washington on 'The Righteous of the World', about non-Jews who had rescued Jews, and our friendship also extended to her home town of Wilkes Barre. I was introduced, and then I could look round for Wiesel. He was deep in conversation with another Nobel Prize winner, Willy Brandt. I was introduced, and then Elie wrote me a few lines for Jacques Attali (the President's *éminence grise*) which introduced me as a member of the committee of the Foundation. He was in the Élysée Palace. How could I get to him?

Carol took me by the hand and escorted me to the palace. When we got into the inner courtyard, where a red carpet was laid out, the band played a march for us. 'They know you,' I told her. She just smiled wanly. Since Chirac was a candidate for the presidency, Mitterand's friends were attempting to exploit this occasion for him. They had told Carol that no press were allowed, that it was to be off the record. But there were French journalists at every corner – only the American journalists were excluded. I wanted to go with Carol to Attali, but she went by herself and came back disappointed. 'He'll think about it,' was the message.

But because I was already in the palace where the first session was to take place, I could at least take part in it that day. So the day and the evening were interesting and stimulating. The only question was how I would get in the next day.

Evelyn always says that I read too many spy novels (like *The Day of the Jackal*, in which someone wants to murder the French President). But one reads in order to learn. How could I penetrate the triple security net and gain entry? I can only say that I saw the flaw in the system straight away. Every morning at 7.30 the big black cars came to pick up the prize winners from the hotel. And every morning at 7.15 I would stand in the hotel lobby and look for a prize winner whom I then accompanied in the car as a friend (holding my Nobel Prize winner's conference briefcase protectively to my chest, where a pass might have been expected). This is almost the best recollection of those days: the cars raced through the streets, against the traffic, along the Champs Elysées, with police on motor-cycles in front of us to make way for us. I nodded to those who wondered or cursed at our way (taxi drivers, for example). The cars went through all the security chains directly into the palace or the Marigny building, for the gathering. In the evening the museums were open to us with amazing formal banquets (the 'jackal' twice shook Mitterand's hand). Then something unexpected happened. Each person had been assigned a place at table. I looked for a place where someone had had to decline – and found my own name. Carol had made it. Now I was legitimate. The game was over. Rather disappointed, next morning I flew back to London.

The critical press did not think this gathering important: too much theatre, too many great hopes. I thought differently. I had heard the speeches, noted the intensive work by really great men and women, and continued to have something of the feeling that I had visited Olympus. Paris was the right place, and it was the right time. Elie Wiesel must in many ways be considered French, though he is also far more. The prophetic and moral element spoke to this group. And it gave me hope for a France which will always remain a land of great possibilities.

How can one describe this gathering?

'Look at them – they really do have an aura of greatness about them,' one of the organizers of the conference said to me. We were standing on the balcony of the Musée d'Orsay, looking down at over seventy Nobel Prize winners wandering through the exhibition of this newest of Paris museums which had been opened that night for a special reception and dinner hosted by President Mitterand and Elie Wiesel. One aspect of Elie Wiesel's dream had been realized: arguably the finest minds in the world had been assembled to discuss the problems of disarmament and peace, human rights, development, science and technology, culture and society. Beyond that, he had hoped to focus attention on the principal moral and political challenges of today, and to evoke imaginative thinking about the future. Part of that vision faded in the long-drawn-out discussions around the conference tables, but in a number of curious ways, the failures themselves were stepping stones towards significant achievements.

The prelude to the conference itself had been a limited, uncertain event: Elie Wiesel had led a number of Nobel Prize winners on a pilgrimage to Auschwitz. The Polish government had given less than full assistance – perhaps because Lech Walesa had been invited and was somehow 'unable to come'. Dialogue had to take place privately. Auschwitz had left its mark upon the visitors. Seated at dinner in the Musée d'Orsay with Mitterand, Willy Brandt, Henry Kissinger and other dignitaries, many of the scholars still found the discussions going back to that moment, again and again.

'Three things about the Auschwitz pilgrimage struck me in particular', said my neighbour on the right. 'First, there was the moment we all stood along the wall of a large building and studied the inscription informing the world that in this place medical experiments were performed upon the inmates. A number of Nobel Prize winners in the field of medicine were among us. I kept wondering about their thoughts. Second – at noon, precisely, a church bell started tolling and tolling. That bell had also rung through the time of destruction. What does that say about the church? About religion?'

'I felt the same things,' replied someone else, 'and I think I know your third impression. Wasn't it the press? Hovering over us, looking for good pictures?'

The first speaker agreed, and listed one more impression which had been shared by the group. Standing some distance from Auschwitz, along the railway track, one could see the entry gate and, on one side of it, a chimney belching out black smoke. That image remained for the pilgrims. They took it into the conference with them, and it entered the atmosphere and ambience with a group of chosen minds who knew that the darkness had not been dispelled, that the twenty-first century would be built upon an age of genocide and cruelty.

The opening session took place at the Salle des Fêtes in the Elysée Palace. There was a moment of silence first, honouring two laureates who had died that week, Sean MacBride and Isidor Rabi, whose wisdom and vision were missed at the meetings. Bruce Kent, president of the International Peace Bureau which won the Peace Prize in 1910, had been at the funeral, and told me of the courageous sermons given by Irish bishops on that day. At the same time, the deep sincerity and quiet dignity of Elie Wiesel made a deep impression on his fellow laureates, and President Mitterand's welcome showed how firmly he supported the aims of the conference. The fact that he had declared his candidacy for another term as President of France the day before was still hard to ignore: the whole apparatus of French bureaucracy had been turned upon the conference. Sadly, this also meant that much of the organization had been taken away from the Elie Wiesel Foundation for Humanity, the sponsoring group, and the French flair for diplomacy was visible by its absence. Special assistants and research scholars invited by Professor Wiesel had their credentials challenged and were turned away from banquets. The Americans had been told that this was a most exclusive, private occasion: no television, etc. As it turned out, the French teams were out in full force, viewing the conference as an election, a media event.

Security was heavy – one Nobel Prize winner, Sir John Eccles, and his wife were taken from the Zurich to Paris train and turned back: they did not have the right visas, only an invitation from the President of France! However, once the conference started, it developed a dynamic of its own. Discomforts and discourtesies were forgotten. The opening concert (Rostropovich, Anne-Sophie Mutter, Bruno Guiranna) and banquet hosted by President Mitterand helped to bring the participants into a happy, communicative situation in which old friendships were renewed and new links were established.

The first morning session was superb. Under Elie Wiesel's direction, five speakers now addressed themselves to the major themes of the conference. The first was Jean Dausset (physics and medicine 1980), whose talk centred upon the explosion of knowledge in our times, and the duties arising out of this. 'We *can* control our destinies,' was his contention, 'but only if we understand the problems.' AIDS was of course the most urgent problem, and he listed the statistics produced by the World Health Organization – between five and ten million in the appreciable future – and the problems which extended beyond medicine into psychology and sociology. Yet the greatest worry, in a way, was in the political area: are registration, segregation and discrimination justified for 'the common good'? Is efficiency the only valid yardstick?

His introduction to genetics and the ability of science to modify genetic codes gave the frightening picture of an alphabet of life – ATCG – where three billion four-letter combinations came to represent humanity, a sentence which could be read (in a million-volume edition), where words became genes. Geneticists, he commented, may be 'sorcerer's apprentices' to their onlookers. Yet he felt that scientists could not and should not limit themselves. However, he did set one limit: one may not modify the embryo – 'that way leads to the gas chamber!' Commenting on this talk, Elie Wiesel stressed the need for human rights within the structure. This led up to the next speaker, Adolfo Perez Esquivel (peace 1980) of the Argentine.

Senor Esquivel spoke with much passion, in his own language. He started from the definition of 'peace' by the Second Vatican Council as the 'creation of justice among men'. 'Peace is preceded by the establishment of justice: personal freedom, where individuals are subjects and not objects of action.' For him, human rights were the instruments through which one achieved freedom. An ethical, critical approach to society could reshape it, and he stressed the need for better housing, food, education, and work. His own experiences in the Argentine, his anger and grief over those who had 'disappeared' in a land torn apart by political violence, led him to link Latin American genocides with permanent violations of social rights which trample individuals and groups under foot. In that connection, he reminded the conference of the Armenians and the Jews, others not to be forgotten in a world where genocide still took place. He felt particular anguish over the eight-year-old Persian Gulf war, the pain of South Africa and Namibia, and stressed particularly the Palestinians and their right to a homeland of their own. He concluded with a strong attack on Reagan's 'Star Wars' and the quotation: 'Leave the stars to lovers – leave them to those who love life!'

William Golding (literature 1983) then shared some short, almost gentle, musings upon the relationship between science and culture. Culture was a way for individuals to multiply their options within their capacities. It was also an attitude towards objects of art and other humans. 'Our humanity is not that of measuring, of weighing. Rather, it is to make value judgments.' And he warned against confusing power with importance.

The star turn was undoubtedly Henry Kissinger (peace 1973), who followed Golding. He challenged his own role as a laureate: he had tried to turn down the award, had sent the money to children orphaned by the Vietnam war, had tried to return the award in 1975. More than anything else, Henry Kissinger felt himself motivated by the awareness that all his classmates in Germany had gone to the concentration camps, and that he himself had lost thirteen members of his family in the camps. Perhaps he was here because he had been one of the few who had really had to confront the question, 'What *can* we do if nuclear war breaks out?' Peace and justice were more than slogans, more than means to an end, and Henry Kissinger tried to define the difference between prophets and politicians.

Prophets deal with absolutes. Politicians deal with contingencies, have to be aware of possible tragedies. Prophets transform the world. Fallible statesmen often set sights too low, and fail for that reason. Yet some statesmen do not fail. And we must come to terms with the fact that peace is not a natural condition and that the statesmen with their accidents reflect our current condition. In his early days at Harvard, Henry Kissinger had already spoken out for arms control and against massive retaliation. The laureates should remember that arms control cannot move forward if there has been no political solution. There must be incentives for both sides to make any reduction possible. And he pointed to the fallacies of certain proposals today, where a 50% reduction had to be related to the difference of 3.8 versus 4.6 of actual warheads which would still be available. Stars for lovers? A beautiful thought which would result in a lack of defences and a climate of fear.

'Why is Mr Gorbachev uneasy?' he asked himself. Perhaps, because he does not know the problems. Statesmen normally discuss issues handed to them by expert technicians who are limited to their own spheres. There must be change. Change creates turmoil and is essential to life. It needs political awareness, which in turn needs compassion. After the year 2000, we will be living in a world with new centres of powers and decision, many of them lacking the moral dimension. And Henry Kissinger turned to Willy Brandt, the Peace Laureate of 1971. It was Brandt who had set up political arrangements in Central Europe at that time which had endured because of their moral content. This must be present in any attempt at reconciliation beween the new alignments confronting us. Not everything can be solved. 'In times when there is turmoil under the heavens,' said Kissinger, 'little problems are dealt with as though they were big problems, and the big problems are not touched on at all. But when order is established, big problems become little, and the little problems disappear!'

It was an optimistic presentation, despite everything.

The final speaker that morning, on economic development, was Professor Lawrence Klein (economics 1980), who had received the award for 'the creation of econometric models and their application to the analysis of economic fluctuations and economic policies'. Applying these insights of both long- and short-term prognoses, he could not give a very optimistic presentation. He concentrated on three issues – hunger, disarmament and debt, particularly the debt of developing countries – and each issue had its dark side. A billion people suffer hunger in our time, an almost unbelievable figure. Searching for hopeful signs, he could point to the green revolution and more liberal agricultural policies. Also, trading of food could lead to the necessary North-South balance, to a more genuine sharing. Here, disarmament could offer economic resources – eventually fifty billion dollars a year – which could bring about such a balance. But Dr Klein gave little hope to the bankers. The mountain of debt was intolerable, and the growing debts would somehow have to be written off. He called for a world conference on debt, at which economic and moral insights might together provde some hope.

The chastened group of laureates then divided into working groups. There it quickly became apparent that there were no simple solutions, and that it was not even possible to arrive at a consensus. The greatest divergences of opinion were in the 'science and technology' group led by Rosalyn Yalow (physiology/medicine 1970) and in the 'disarmament and peace' group led by Dr John Polanyi (chemistry 1986). The differences were predictable and need not be detailed here: 'hard' versus 'soft' options, general statements versus firm proposals. In the peace group, Henry Kissinger won the respect but not the assent of his opponents. Some wanted to make radical proposals in the political arena, like Bruce Kent of the International Peace Bureau; by contrast, Mairead Corrigan Maguire and Betty Perkins (1977 Nobel Peace Prize for their Community of Peace People in Northern Ireland) simply wanted people to 'love one another'. And the scientists – confronted by such unscientific thinking – generally opted for caution. This division became apparent in all of the discussions which followed, and it might be argued that the general statements which emerged at the end, with all their poetry and moral fervour, amounted to an admission that a one-week conference of the great minds of our time cannot offer any solutions in our time of suffering. The admission must be made. It does not mean that the conference was a failure. It succeeded, but in ways which will only become apparent in the future...

The conference itself, this dream of Elie Wiesel's, moved from being a vision to being a reality. The psychological, sociological, political and even spiritual dimensions in all their complexities led to a structure which deserves the closest study. Of course this structure had weaknesses. The gods had descended fom Olympus, from their own world where they were accustomed to domination and unquestioned support. Suddenly, there were seventy of them, each a super-star. They were no longer alone at the top. I ventured to disagree mildly with a physicist who considered Reagan too liberal. How dared I! An onlooker who had not even come down from Mount Olympus – her own rabbi supported her fully! And I was

expelled from this laureate's orbit. Yet this was the exception
to the rule. The greater the person, the more accessible he or
she was. It was the openness, the readiness to enter into
discussion, the club-like atmosphere of this most exclusive club
in the world, which dominated after a while. Old friendships
and cordial oppositions were renewed, and new relationships
were established, If some groups congregated in corners of the
Marigny to discuss field particles as communicators of weak
interactions (!), others engaged in interdisciplinary confron-
tations. Fears were communicated; and hopes. It was possible
to address moral issues, and to find strength in the vision of
others.

One of the decisions made at the end of the conference was
to create an emergency committee which could intervene with
moral authority in whatever crisis situations might arise. And
they decided to meet again in two years, under the auspices of
the Elie Wiesel Foundation for Humanity, in New York. No
major policy statements were made; no solutions to the most
urgent problems of our time. A certain number of conclusions
were offered, stressing the need to turn to reason in times of
emotional turmoil: 'the gap which exists in many countries
between political power and the intellectual community should
be narrowed... education should be the absolute priority of all
national budgets...', statements which led the London papers
(*The Independent*, 22 January) to view the group as the voice of
intellect: 'The self-fertilization of eggheads seems to be some
way ahead of embryo reseach!' That paper also traced the
minimal support for disarmaaent: '...it might make some more
money available for economic and social development'... to
'the shadowy influence of Dr Henry Kissinger'. The same issue
of *The Independent* also muttered that 'the proceedings of the
conference have been shrouded in secrecy', but that some
laureates had had more influence on the meeting than others
– not a startling insight.

The fact is that Elie Wiesel dominated the conference and its
deliberations, and forced the scientists to open their disciplines
to the moral quesions present in scientific decisions. 'The
sciences are always attacked for being immoral,' one of the
laureates complained, but the decisions of the scientists

assembled stressed the ethical dimension above all else. In his concluding remarks, Elie Wiesel stressed the moral conclusions reached, calling for a world conference on debt for the pooling of resources into AIDS rather than a dispersal of efforts by different pharmacetuical concerns. And the conference turned back towards the beginning, the awareness of a heritage of brutality and barbarism which must not be taken into the next century. Suddenly, one saw again the small group of laureates standing at the gates of Auschwitz, where science had been suborned and where humanity had lost its way. At this moment – indeed throughout this five-day dialogue with one another – they remembered the past in order to find a way towards the future.

The Prophet Elisha in Neuwied

There is a quite special partnership between me and Pastor Jürgen Seim: I write letters to the teachers of former times, and he replies in their names. That came about quite without any preparation, completely unplanned. In 1983, the Luther quincentenary, I was asked for a contribution on 'Martin Luther through the eyes of a Jew' for a radio series. That was the origin of the talk 'When Brother Martin threw his ink-pot at me', which has been published many times since. A reply appeared in a book, Brother Martin's letter to Brother Albert, written by Jürgen Seim. Even in his children's stories he found himself on the same way to Leo Baeck as I did. That led to a friendship which has been strengthened by many visits, a real dialogue.

Now I was with him in Neuwied again. My lecture to his congregation and his colleagues was on our work together in seeking to understand the darkest time of our life. As we had done so often before, this time we also began with a Bible study. Holocaust and Bible come together in the attempt to understand human suffering in the world. Twenty years ago my textbook on the Holocaust, *Out of the Whirlwind: The Literature of the Holocaust*, appeared in the United States. As an introduction I had used a story which Elie Wiesel had passed on to me along with much loving advice. It was the story of the prophet Elijah, who went up to heaven in a chariot of fire – here, as a fugitive from Auschwitz who warned his fellow believers and then returned to the camp, to ascend in the cloud of fire. As a postscript to this text I wrote the story of Elijah's disciple, the prophet Elisha, which was based on the Hebrew texts. When I visited Neuwied, this story was the introduction to our meeting.

After some time Jürgen sent me a new text, a sermon for his congregation. In it the Jewish story was extended to Christianity and renewed. This kind of dialogue justifies my journey into this time, so the story should now find a place in this book:

A chariot of fire and Israel's body as smoke through the air.

A parable by Albert Friedlander.

The prophet Elijah recognized that the time had come. A chariot of fire with fiery horses would come and take him to heaven. The disciples already withdrew and saw him no more. Only Elisha went with his master into the wilderness. 'Stay with the others, go back,' the prophet told him. 'My difficult way continues, and I shall never complete the work. The mantle of a prophet hangs heavy on one's shoulders. What do you want with it? Go back!'

Elisha shook his head and followed his master.

The time was near.

'Ask what I should do for you before I am taken from you,' said Elijah to Elisha.

'Let me have a twofold portion, the portion of the firstborn, of your spirit,' said the disciple.

'It is difficult to give it, and more difficult to receive it,' said Elijah. 'It will happen if you see the chariot of fire, but not otherwise.'

A path of fire opened up to heaven, and Israel's body ascended in the smoke through the air. The tree of time shook, and a star stopped singing. Was it a chariot of fire or was it six million? Was there a witness? Elisha had not turned away his eyes. He saw it. And his suffering cried aloud into the night: 'My father! My father! The chariots of Israel and its horsemen!'

Then he saw him no more. He seized his garments and tore them in two pieces. He stumbled through the wilderness, fell over stones – or were they children's shoes? He found the black mantle which had fallen from Elijah, and a great rage came over him.

Elijah took the mantle, struck the water with it, like Moses, like his teacher Elijah, and said: 'Where is now the Lord, the

God of Elijah?' And the Jordan divided on both sides so that he could pass through. He told the story to the others – great unbelief. Some small groups went out to look. They looked for the dust which glittered at the end of the universe. They had not seen the chariot of fire. They knew nothing. It was the task of Elisha to tell them what had been lost, and what had now to be done. The waters of their knowledge were disturbed. They brought him a shell for his salt tears. He shook it into the springs of their knowledge, and the springs became clear. Elisha took over the place of Elijah.

He was not a good prophet. Elijah had stood high above the rest; his fire and his power had brought them to him, had put them on the way. Elisha was one of them, in the midst of the group. The shadow of Elijah hung over them like a black mantle. Elijah's cup was filled on every Seder evening; his chair stood ready at every circumcision; his place was secure in the hope of his people. They knew that Elijah would come again, in the messianic time, even before the Messiah.

But Elisha had seen him go, had seen the chariot of fire. As soon as he recognized this moment of his life, he again became strong enough to bear the mantle. He would never become the great leader of the people. But he could be one of them, could be a witness in their midst. He kept talking to them about the chariot of fire, showed them the smoke which went through the air. He lived his testimony.

'My father,' he wept, 'my father! O, the chariot of fire!'

There are some who say that the Messiah cannot come until the time when people stop asking about Elijah and begin to hear the testimony of Elisha. The messianic way – it once appeared to the patriarch Jacob in his dream as a golden ladder – was torn up and burned by the chariots of fire of our time. Once the ladder was built from heaven down to earth. But now it must rise from earth to heaven, and people must take part in its building. This will only happen when the whispered dark testimony is accepted in the midst of humanity. The many must see and recognize the way of the chariot of fire. Mourning and loss must be experienced by day and by night. They must weep over the burnt-out past and must look upon the ashes of the future. The way of fire must be stamped on their understanding, the way of fire into the darkness. Their lips must compel them with trembling and torment to say the words which can create the beginning of a golden ladder:

Yitgadal v'yitkadash sh'me rabba – Exalted and hallowed be the great name.

They say that this prayer has to be repeated six million times. But people have forgotten why that should be so.

A sermon by Jürgen Seim

At the beginning of the history of Israel there is a ladder which joins heaven and earth. Jacob, who was given the name Israel at that time, dreamed of the union of heaven and earth. In his dream God made a bond with Jacob, with Israel, with the world. From then on there is the messianic hope that earth will be joined with heaven, that God and man will belong together, that we here and he there will be together in the mystery and under the commandment, when he says, 'I am the Lord your God', and, 'You shall have no other gods but me.'

The prophet Elijah belongs in the story of this messianic hope. In Jewish memory he is the great prophetic figure, in lonely exaltation above the others alongside Moses. On those of his people who turned away from God, who simply forgot him, who did not want to be disturbed by him, on these people he again, continually, impressed the first commandment. He addressed them in the name of the God who had revealed his name to them, led them out of slavery in Egypt, and given them his commandments. He hammered home to them that they are God's people, because he is their God, and that they are to respond to his loyalty with their loyalty. The life-story of Elijah is governed by the messianic hope that God and his people belong together; and by mourning, because they are not together. With this hope and this mourning he towers above the history of the Jewish people, down to the present day. When they celebrate the passover, but also at other festivals, they keep a place for Elijah and pour a cup of wine for him. For since the short prophetic writing of Malachi, the hope has been that Elijah will return before the day of the Lord comes, before the Messiah comes (Mal.3.23).

Albert Friedlander has taken the story of Elijah's farewell and has related it to the history of the suffering of the people of Israel in our century. The parable is both concentrated and wider-ranging. It embraces thousands of years, far-ranging hope and penetrating sorrow. It is a Jewish composition, not a Christian one. We do not appear in it, despite its wide scope. But when we listen to it, we learn something of the God of Israel, in whom we also believe. If it is true, as Albert Friedlander says, that Jews and Christians live in one covenant, then we can learn the messianic hope anew from this work, Christians as well as Jews: from the foundations, again from an abyss.

Albert Friedlander recalls the narrative of Elijah's farewell. The old prophet goes through the land with Elisha, his pupil and prophet-to-be. There is a tacit expectation among all in the land, as if the history of Israel were at a turning point, as if all the clocks had been stopped. Mourning extends over the parting of the great prophet, who had reminded people so authoritatively of God. Against this sorrow the hope is to stand fast that God remains bound to his people and thus to the world. Elijah's place will be empty only until the Messiah comes.

Just as God once built Jacob the ladder which joined heaven and earth, so he sends for Elijah the chariot of fire with the fiery horses, which take him from earth to heaven, into the divine mystery.

But this fiery way to heaven evokes another fresh memory, that of the burning ovens from which 'Israel's body ascended in smoke through the air', as the poet Nelly Sachs said ('O you chimneys'). What now? Was it a chariot of fire or was it six million? Where does the mesianic hope remain in the face of this unfathomable sorrow?

First of all there is Elisha's cry of lament: 'My father, our protector, the chariots of Israel and its horsemen!' Elisha takes up the mantle of Elijah. Now he is the prophet with the whole burden of the task of proclaiming both mourning and hope. He has to go back to the others; he stumbles over the stones in the wilderness; but perhaps he also stumbles over the shoes of those children who have been gassed, murdered. He is fearfully alone, a witness to the shining ascension which no one can believe. The others to whom he returns know nothing. The miraculous fiery way of Elijah is incomprehensible, and so is the dreadful fiery way of Israel. Elisha is to utter the incomprehensible. Only through his sorrow will they begin to guess how much sorrow and how much unfulfilled hope stands between God and Israel. Here he is no great prophet like Elijah. He does not stand like Elijah high above the others, but lives in their midst. But he bears witness to what he has seen. In the face of unbelief he speaks of the chariot of fire and smoke. No notice is taken of him; Elijah is expected as the forerunner of the Messiah. But, Albert Friedlander asks in his parable, is there still reason to hope, where the ladder of Jacob's dream is torn down and burned by the chariots of fire in our time? Can Israel look for Elijah, in order to expect the Messiah after him? Must it not rather listen to the bitter testimony of Elisha, which would mean sharing in his sorrow? He says that once upon a time the ladder was built from heaven down to earth so that God could be united with his people and his world. Now, he says, since the ladder has been torn down and burned, it must rise from earth to heaven, and human beings must take part in its building.

To Christian ears that sounds as though someone wants to do what only God can do: unite heaven and earth. But if I understand him rightly, he does not mean that, because that cannot be. He means something different: mourning and loss must be experienced day and night. He asserts in bewilderment that the bond between God and the world is destroyed by nothing other than human guilt, and that now the many, Jews and Christians and Gentiles, go on by day and sleep by night as though nothing had happened. He sees Elisha standing there as a witness to sorrow and hope, and wishes for himself and his people and the world that the whispered dark testimony may be accepted in the midst of humanity; that the farewell of the one Elijah and the murderous farewell of the six million may be noted. The testimony of the fiery way, shining from Elijah and blazing from the Jews, should be impressed on the life of all of us.

The ladder from earth to heaven, the new bond – that would be the deepest sorrow over the way in which the ladder from heaven to earth, the original bond, has been torn down and burnt.

The Jewish prayer for the dead, the Kaddish, begins, 'Exalted and hallowed be the great name'. God himself is said to be present in sorrow, his name is said to be exalted and hallowed. The Kaddish, the prayer for the dead, would be the beginning of building the ladder, praying to make the connection with God, building up a hope in and against sorrow.

In his parable Albert Friedlander says that this prayer, the Kaddish, has to be repeated six million times, for none of the dead of Israel may remain unmourned. He expresses his fear that people will forget to say Kaddish. He tells the sad parable of the fiery way of Elijah and Israel to rouse us to sorrow and hope. In his poem he is near enough to reality to say that there is no hope without sorrow, that only unawareness is also lack of sorrow – just as Elijah's contemporaries did not understand anything and the waters of their knowledge were disturbed. Only when he poured in a shell, filled with his salt tears for his great father Elijah, did the springs of their knowledge become clear.

The age-old story of Elijah's farewell helps the rabbi today in his writing to come close to the suffering of Israel, and then from the depths of the sorrow to arrive at the breadth of hope, as by Jacob's golden ladder.

To begin with, we Christians can only listen to this. We can acknowledge our share of guilt. We can begin to understand how the suffering of Jesus is interwoven with Jewish suffering. We can accept the whispered dark testimony. Because we are in a covenant with Israel because of Jesus, we can take part in the mourning, and then perhaps also in the messianic hope.

And the Music Plays On

'The rabbi is wanted on the telephone.'

The group looked at me sympathetically. After a good dinner we were sitting in the living room and chatting about everything under the sun, but not about pastoral calls. It could just as well have been the doctor, and some business people also had these little bleepers in their pockets which could call them to work at any time. But so late in the evening...

'The man says that it's urgent.'

I already knew. 'Put on Capital Radio,' I told my friends, 'it could be interesting.' I went into another room and picked up the telephone. I immediately heard the well-known voice, which was not speaking directly to me.

'This is Louis Alexander for the night programme. Many questions have already been sent in for our three wise men – Bishop Hugh Montefiore, Monsignor Bruce Kent and Rabbi Friedlander. The first question is about the problem of the Near East and the readiness of Israel to hit back. The question is: isn't this the old Hebrew principle of vengeance: an eye for an eye, a tooth for a tooth? What do you think, Rabbi Friedlander?'

In a lecture I would have given a full explanation of the *lex talionis* and demonstrated that the biblical law was a limitation of the blood vengeance of the ancient Near East, that it was really meant to replace the *value* of the eye or the tooth – but in a radio conversation one doesn't have much time. And this was a radio conversation. To get the three of us on the programme, Louis had shown us that we wouldn't even have to give up any time. He could always make a telephone connection, and as on this evening I could even ask questions of the questioner, could examine his prejudices and convince if not him, then perhaps the audience, that the problems of the state of Israel could not simply be explained by the 'principle of vengeance'. Twenty minutes later I returned to my friends.

'That was a surprise,' they conceded, 'but don't think that you've finished. The answer to the third question about women rabbis wasn't right. We wanted to telephone – but you were on the telephone. However, now...' And the conversation went on late into the night.

There are so many possibilities of collaborating with colleagues, attacking prejudices and bearing witness to one's own tradition. Radio and television keep robbing us of time to learn, but they are also an important sphere of work. Since I've lived in England I've often found myself in a studio to discuss religious problems. The BBC is always extremely fair about letting the Jewish voice be heard. Nevertheless there are difficulties. The Orthodox regularly complain that one hears only the liberal Reform rabbis: Lionel Blue, Julia Neuberger, Hugo Gryn, John Rayner and occasionally me. But our group also complains. We once decided that all our rabbis should have training for radio and television so that they could share this honour. Many people now have a diploma (we five don't have) and are waiting for the call. It doesn't come. A new generation of younger rabbis has grown up: Jonathan Magonet, Danny Smith, Alexandra Wright; but Orthodoxy has only a few voices in this area, perhaps because people are more closed to the outside world.

For me the media became a possible way of encountering people and ideas which broadened my faith, but also led me into quite a new area.

Music.

You also need to know that I am the only completely unmusical person in my family. At the age of eleven Evelyn gave a concert in the London Festival Hall; after studying at the Royal College of Music she wanted to become a pianist, but then she married me... Our three daughters have inherited her gift, so I am the only one who cannot even read music.

I became a librettist.

That happened slowly, almost imperceptibly. The composer Samuel Adler, Professor at the Eastman School of Music, had invited me to a summer school for Jewish students in Great Barrington, Massachusetts. We became friends, and I asked him to look after a lovely girl, Carol Stalker, one of the students. I went to England, met Evelyn and immediately fell in love. Sam married Carol. As a kind of wedding present I translated the text of a cantata on Abraham and Isaac by his father, but had to alter some things and make additions. This work by Sam, *The Binding*, was a great success. And then, through a radio programme in a London cathedral, I met Donald Swann. He had become famous through his work with Michael Flanders. *At the Drop of A Hat* and *At the Drop of Another Hat* had been very successful in London and New York: everyone knew some of the songs. Nowadays they are taught in school. Flanders sat in his wheelchair and Donald Swann at the piano, and a whole decade loved their works, in the style of Noel Coward. Flanders was the librettist and Swann the composer. Then they parted, and Donald became more involved with religion, though he continued to accompany singers and composed new songs. Now he wanted to write a religious work, *The Four Seasons*. He began with autumn and invited me to write a Jewish text that would fit it.

In the autumn we read the book of Ecclesiastes in the synagogue, and I took this book, along with an old story which occurs in Judaism and also outside: the story of the two brothers. They live side by side and one is married. At harvest time they both think: I have more than enough and my brother has too little. In the night each fills his brother's storehouse, until one night they meet on their fields and embrace. 'At this place,' the rabbis say, 'the temple was built.' Nowadays, one must say the Al Aqsa Mosque, the Temple Wall and the Church of the Sepulchre stand on this place – our work on text and music became a plea for brotherhood.

After this beginning other works developed: *The Harp and the Lover*, about the Song of Songs; *Esther* became a winter tale; *The Destroyed Cities, Lamentations*, spoke of the hot hatred of a summer heatwave; and *Ruth* became the fifth season, the messianic time, and combined Jewish and Christian ideas of hope. Together these five parts became a cantata which Donald performed in many cities, in England, but also in Nairobi, in

America and in Israel. The texts were all held together by a narrator – naturally I had written them for Evelyn. So she went on tour with Donald. It was, and continued to be, a sermon which Donald and Evelyn and the choir gave in a variety of churches, synagogues and universities, in 1989 even at the Brighton Festival. It is to be performed once again in Israel, and Donald and I tried to get an Arab-Jewish children's choir for the performance. They told us that we were being premature. But this *must* come about one day.

'Can you write a hymn for the wedding of Charles and Diana?', I was asked by Malcolm Williamson, Master of the Queen's Music. I doubted it, but the opportunity to work with him was a great honour. Malcolm loved his Jewish fellow-citizens, and Dolly, his wife (now divorced) was a member of my congregation. He very much wanted English Jewry to share in the wedding in this way. But things were too complicated. Many people did not know that this wedding was 'private' and not public. That meant, for example, that Charles, the Prince of Wales, could give preference to his own Principality and therefore commission the wedding hymn from a Welsh composer. That hurt Malcolm Williamson, but as the royal composer he nevertheless wanted to give the couple a song, and it seemed to him to be right and proper for this to be a present from the English Jews. And so I wrote a hymn, which was based on the Song of Solomon: the entry of the royal bridegroom into Jerusalem.

In this collaboration I learned a very great deal from Malcolm. Donald accepted my texts without alterations and wrote the music very easily, in the shortest time. Malcolm Williamson needed more time, and it became quite clear that the music was the most important thing. We sat together at Evelyn's Blüthner, and he asked a good deal more of me. 'These words don't fit the music, change the text... at this point I need another image, change the text... I want five lines for each verse, change...'

I admired him. There are so many difficulties in his life and so little success. He suffers. His music is often delayed, and it is recognized more in his home country of Australia. But we finished our hymn and presented it to the bridal couple. I had heard it only on tape; the premiere was in Melbourne. But now when there is a wedding in our synagogue, I sometimes suggest, 'How about the royal wedding hymn...?' There is, however, a slight change – I allowed myself to be convinced by our cantor Harold Lester, and now we have only two of the five verses of the hymn at a wedding. I like all five, but I recognize that not all music lovers share my views.

The most difficult work in this area was the requiem, *Kaddish for Terezin*, with Ronald Senator, which was performed for the first time to a congregation of a thousand people in Canterbury Cathedral in 1986. It had been brought to birth at a dark time. Evelyn, Ronald and I were sitting at the deathbed of his wife Dita. We all loved her very much. Dita was in Terezin as a child and was then sent to Auschwitz and survived. She had a happy marriage with Ronald. They lived in a commune, 'Fabyc', 'Family by choice'. Dita had cancer; she was very brave and was more concerned about Ronald. When she died, we knew that we had to do something to honour her memory. Evelyn made the first suggestion which eventually led to this requiem: a song for the children of Terezin. A million children died in the death camps, an incomprehensible number which I have to think of again and again. And so I wrote the requiem.

In my textbook about the Holocaust, and also in my liturgical works, I try to use as much as possible of the writing of those involved. Only they were the witnesses; only they may be the witnesses. The children in Terezin wrote poems, diaries, painted pictures. I used that for the libretto, and also poems by Paul Celan and Nelly Sachs, both specially witnesses and great poets of our time.

I took the text to Ronald Senator. Like Malcolm Williamson, he did some more work on it and gave me new poems which he wanted to work into the music – laughing, joking poems, to show that there was more than the dark night (a lovely, funny song about a cat, for example). Ronald is a gifted composer, whose works range from symphonies to operas for children. He wrote the requiem for orchestra, male choir, children's choir and – a shophar. Our friend Hugo Gryn, who went through Auschwitz with his dying father, was the shophar blower and the narrator. I had also written this text for Evelyn. but the performance was costing too much money for the B'nai B'rith music festival, and they wanted a 'well-known name', i.e. Rabbi Gryn. Hugo wanted to give way for Evelyn, but B'nai B'rith refused, and I gave in. I'm still grateful to Hugo for this. The requiem had to be performed, but part of the text needed a woman's voice. However, when it came to the performance in the Lincoln Center, B'nai B'rith again insisted on a well-known name, and James Leroy Jones was signed up. A children's choir from Harlem was rehearsed. And then there were more problems with money. The performance was to be moved to the cathedral, but at the last moment B'nai B'rith withdrew the 30,000 dollars that they had promised – on the grounds that they had already given away too much that year. Had that happened earlier, we would have got the money from elsewhere – but this premiere collapsed, and the requiem was not performed in America until 1988.

In Canterbury it was a great experience of all of us. All the problems were solved, including those which arose for religious reasons. For example, in New York B'nai B'rith did not want to use the Latin prayers from the Christian liturgy, because Orthodox Jews would be opposed to them. But Christian children also died in Terezin. And some Orthodox Jews in the choir insisted that the name of God should not be pronounced in the Hebrew prayers. We showed understanding towards one another, and the requiem in the cathedral meant a great deal to the Jews and Christians who heard it. The dean of the cathedral gave a short introduction – for me it was and remains a shared experience of suffering, which had to lead us into a new religious encounter.

The requiem was performed the same year in Jerusalem, and in the next year also in America. I think that it was also a comfort for Ronald. His life without Dita was dark, but this work gave him the possibility of living again. Now he had married an American pianist, Miriam – I married them in my synagogue, and I am delighted at their happiness today. I have great hopes for their shared career in New York. Dita remains in our life: my daughter Ariel and I both wrote poems which were also a prayer for her. The real heart of the requiem also remains in my life – it is a Kaddish, a prayer of remembrance for the children, all of whom are to go on living through us.

The premiere in Canterbury was also broadcast on the radio, and many people wrote or telephoned afterwards, to express their gratitude. I often play the cassette, late in the evening, when I am at home and continuing to work in this area; when I am all alone and when I remember how alone the children where. And I am grateful to Ronald.

Master Death Visits Basle

It was a hot summer day, and I was back in Basle again. I always enjoy being in Basle, despite my experiences. My first visit there remains unforgettable. I was to give a lecture at Herder Verlag in Freiburg, and flew from London to Basle. As an experienced traveller I had only a small briefcase with me in the plane and was first off it. So I was first in the hall, first through passport control and snapped up the only taxi outside. 'Station please,' and away we went.

I regarded the poor travellers who were now coming through the door with some sympathy, made myself comfortable in the car and studied my manuscript. The journey was taking quite a long time. After twenty minutes I became disturbed and asked, 'How much longer to Basle station?' 'Monsieur, you're in France. We're going to Mulhouse.' I had stumbled out of the French exit into the taxi.

On the journey from Mulhouse to Basle I had an opportunity to practise humility, and I was much more modest when I finally arrived in Freiburg, of course too late for the evening meal. The paper suffered somewhat under this pressure.

This time I made no mistake, but I had a good deal on my mind. Evelyn's uncle sought to escape from the Nazis into Switzerland, and succeeded in crossing the border in 1940. But then he was caught by the Swiss frontier police. They were very friendly, first gave him a cup of coffee and then a decent meal. (However, they were only waiting for the result of a call to Germany: 'We have a Jew for you,' they said to their German colleagues.) Two hours later, everything had been settled. They sent him back over the border, and he died in Auschwitz.

The Swiss 'lifeboat'... I know there were reasons, neutrality

113

had to be preserved... 'one' had to be sacrificed for 'many', and so on. But the picture of this adventurous young man is over the fireplace in our London home – and stands between me and Switzerland. When I really saw Basle for the first time, on the way back from Freiburg, there was something dark there. I encountered death in Basle.

That was quite natural. I visited the hospital in which my teacher Selma Stern-Täubler was spending the last days of her life. Deep stillness. A great goodness and much trust in life surrounded her; here death was not an enemy, but a natural ingredient of life. When I was a student in Cincinnati, Selma Stern-Täubler and Eugen Täubler were almost my parents. Their home in Riddle Road was only a few steps away from Hebrew Union College, and I went to see them every week. Selma corrected my dissertation on the 'Association for the Culture and Science of Judaism'. Even now, in the last days of her life, she again came to speak of Jewish history. Her fundamental work on the Jews in Prussia is and remains a monument, but this afternoon we spoke mostly about her favourite figure in Jewish history, Josel von Rosheim, the 'Commander' of the Jews in Germany (a title which I also gave Leo Baeck in my biography). *Stadlanut*, representation of Judaism by a prominent figure who had access to those in power, was the normal link between the Jewish minority and the state in which it lived; Selma Stern's work also showed the problems and dark sides of this connection. Her great book on the court Jews made us recognize the tragedy of Jewish destiny at a time when a few capable people were attempting to find a way out of the ghetto into the world outside. At the time of parting Selma Stern remained my teacher and foster-mother. We kissed good-bye, and then I returned to London. With great calmness she welcomed friendly death in Basle.

My last visit but one to Basle brought me a similar encounter. However, this was not a sad experience, but sheer joy in the sunlight. Evelyn, our daughter Noam and I were visiting an old lady who was still so lively and open that all the boundaries of age were crossed. Fritzi welcomed us into her house, entertained us to coffee and cakes which were so good that they reminded us of the past, and told us something of her problems with publishers and the television. She was anxious that a television series which was soon to appear in London might distort the family history. Frau Frank, the widow of Otto Frank, felt responsible for rescuing the true heritage of Anne Frank from attacks. She had survived Auschwitz, and before the war had long been a friend of the Frank family; she knew Anne very well. When Otto Frank was the only member of the family to survive, they met. But something remarkable then happened: Otto Frank was begrudged this autumn of a new love and family joy. He had become a symbol, Anne Frank's father, a figure in *The Diary of Anne Frank*, in the film, on the stage. He devoted his whole life to looking after the Anne Frank Foundation, he answered each of the thousand letters which were written to him by the readers of Anne Frank's diary. But this was not enough for the world. He was to be an unchanging monument of stone, without developing further. Otto and Fritzi left Amsterdam and made a peaceful new life for themselves in Basle.

Our work in the World Union for Progressive Judaism had brought us together often. Shortly after the war I visited Amsterdam for the first time and Otto Frank showed me everything: the hiding place, the other homes in which Jews found lodging, the memorial to the transport workers who refused to drive Jews to Germany, and much else. When Meyer Levin began the great controversy over the dramatization of the diary, I tried to mediate in some way, but that didn't work. Evelyn and I also met Otto in London and Paris, and we valued his friendship greatly. Some time previously the Anne Frank exhibition had come to London, so there were new encounters with the family. My synagogue became the depot for the exhibition when it was not on the road, and I took part in the opening. That was important, because there was an attempt – from the Jewish side – to organize a kind of boycott: the politician Ken Livingstone had made himself responsible for the exhibition. Since he was very left-wing and supported Palestinians and minorities, there was a fear that Anne Frank and the Holocaust would simple become a pretext for left-wing criticism of the state. The boycott failed, but I was almost the only 'prominent' Jew to take part in the opening ceremony. So we had a new encounter. We were all anxious that day about how the hateful attacks on the authenticity of the diary would develop, and how the television play about Anne Frank would be received in England. Of course the attacks came to nothing, and the television play was not bad (I was not enthusiastic, but I have to concede that each generation has the right to understand this story in its own way).

Basle, another encounter with a good woman.

But on this hot summer's day in 1988 I was only travelling through, on my way to Zurich, to the Leipman Agency and Eva Koralnik. She looks after my books and it was my first visit. When I entered the building I immediately saw a cupboard with the Anne Frank books in all languages. I had not known that this agency handles them. So I immediately felt at home.

In my thoughts I was still in Basle. Crossing the frontier had made me sad, because I again thought of 'Bubi', Evelyn's uncle. Crossing frontiers always disturbs me – one puts oneself in the hands of the authoritites, even if the frontiers in Europe are hardly frontiers any more. I had tried that out the previous year. After the Katholikentag in Aachen, where I had to give a lecture, I had to get back to London quickly for a solemn evening service. The quickest and cheapest connection was through Maastricht. But something unpleasant happened: on the Friday morning, two hours before the departure of the plane, a pickpocket enriched himself with my passport, and there was no time then to take up the matter with the police. A pretty girl was prepared to drive me to Maastricht (the adjective is important).

'Good,' I said, 'and when we get to the frontier, drive very slowly. Don't stop. Just wave and give them a friendly smile.' She waved and smiled, the frontier police waved back, and we were in Holland. In Maastricht I checked in my small bag (if they turned me back, all the luggage would have to be unloaded again). Fifteen minutes before the flight I 'discovered' that I didn't have my passport, and reported the fact to the police. 'But how did you get over the frontier?' the policeman at the airport wanted to know. I explained the waving and smiling. 'So that's how we fight terrorism,' he said gloomily.

'Will that cause any difficulties with my flight?' I asked.

'What do you think?' he replied, 'We are deporting you. We insist on your taking the flight. The people at Gatwick can deal with the problem.'

In Gatwick I was sent into a waiting room, although I told them that I was an American with permission to reside in England and that my name was in the telephone book. The room was full of people from the Third World, and feelings of guilt came over me – I guessed what would happen. And so it was: after ten minutes I was called back to the window. The official told me that he had the right to believe a story or not, and they believed mine. I went through the barrier and looked back. There they still sat, anxious, resigned, annoyed. For them the frontier was too high.

The Swiss still have their frontiers, but now they're more lax. And for those who want to travel to Switzerland without a passport, I have to describe this experience with the frontier, a tip from my experiences on my last trip. You take the IC train from Freiburg to Basle-Baden station. You don't leave the station, don't go through customs, but look for the platform where the train to the Swiss station stops (a four-minute journey). No passport control! Now you're in Switzerland and you take the train to Zurich. It's the same procedure on the way back, and my passport didn't see the light of day. If only things had been like that in 1940!

In Zurich I went first to the Hotel Storchen, a kind of pilgrimage in memory of the meeting which Nelly Sachs had with Paul Celan at this place. Celan's poem speaks of the 'quarrelling patience' which existed between him and God. Paul Celan's presence in my London home, my visit to Nelly Sachs in Stockholm, were reminiscences which revived again here. I drank my coffee and tried to put myself into the conversation which Nelly Sachs and Paul Celan had had here. The letters between the two of them, above all the gloomy intimations which Celan expressed in one of these letters to her, could make one believe that this was a melancholy encounter. But other things tell against that: the place, the lake, the sun, the view of the cathedral as Celan's poem describe them – all that must have made this hour an extension of their life. And I recalled another poem, quite unknown (it was only

117

duplicated for friends), which Eugen Täubler wrote in 1936. Perhaps he too was sitting here with a friend.

> Jerusalem... Zurich
> We were wine, and our dry power
> filled the glass to the very brim...
> It had ripened in a distant land.

> So we are held, like wine in glass, in thrall,
>   by the consistency of gleaming light;
>   the mass of primal being strives to form itself,

> tautens itself within to being never seen
> Whose in the wine – and whose in us the power?

(Eugen Täubler, *Umbra Vitae*, 1936, p.6).

The one cup of coffee did not give me a permanent seat in the Hotel zum Storchen. After a while I left the table and a taxi took me to the Liepman agency. We went by the cemetery where James Joyce is buried and I honoured Leopold and Molly Bloom with a fleeting thought – one can't keep getting off the subject. Soon after that, Eva Koralnik and I were working on the plans for this book and for further work in an area in which I encounter the cruelty of the past. But, after travelling through the valley of the shadow of death, I am open to fellow human beings and their love. Eva wanted to call Fritzi for me, but I hesitated. I had other appointments in Basle that afternoon which I did not want to change. Afterwards I was sorry. It's always a mistake to put off conversations and meetings until later. In August I had been in East Hampton, New York and telephoned Hannah Tillich. We had a good conversation, but she had a cold, so we promised ourselves a long visit the next time. There was no next time; Hannah Tillich died a few months later.

The Holbein exhibition was on at this time in Basle, his sketches and preliminary work for most of his best-known works. Holbein died in London, in the Black Death, and we had admired many of his paintings which are in the Queen's possession in Windsor Castle. When I returned to Zurich,

Evelyn and our daughter Noam were in the Museum to renew their love for this great painter. Here one could recognize the real man behind the court clothing, a way inwards without words. But I was making my particular way back to Freiburg – without a passport. I had seen too many pictures over the last months. Dr Elisabeth Maxwell was compiling a major exhibition with paintings done in the concentration camps for a conference in London and Oxford and she asked me to look at the pictures and use them in my next book. These were pictures from another Black Death which showed people in the deepest distress, including the monsters who had put themselves in the innermost circle of hell. Suffering and fear cry out from each prisoner's face, but also their humanity. In the other faces there is just brutality.

Art is also a prayer in human life. In the liturgy we find praise and accusations, a cry of distress, a thanksgiving for the blessings of life. They say that in the Ten Commandments (Thou shalt not make any graven image), Judaism set itself against art, but this is a misunderstanding. Anyone looking at a Jewish book with its calligraphy or the art in the synagogue or in a Jewish house will know that here art is loved, only it is not to be worshipped. It is a barrier against brutality and barbarism. It is a claim on *simcha*, on joy, the recognition of how much God has given human beings. In the Torah we find the artist Bezalel, whose works are built on *chochmah*, on the knowledge and recognition of the divine plan. It has always been the barbarians who have destroyed art, in Rome as in Jerusalem: it was a brutal group of Roman soldiers (under the command of the emperor) who set the temple on fire. Brutality destroys art or brings it down to its own level, as one can see in the paintings of the Nazi period.

Even religion can be infected by this disease of barbarism. In Basle, for example, where many of Holbein's finest paintings were torn up and burned, one can learn that religion too becomes barbaric when it sets itself against art. The term 'degenerate art' derives from the Hitler period (what could one expect of an amateur when he comes to power?), but any dictatorship fears art – it speaks too directly to people. Therefore I found it particularly interesting that this year the DDR was

119

allowing exhibitions which did not correspond at all to Socialist realism. People wandered quite baffled through a hall – looking at shopping bags. I sought the philosophy behind this art. An attack on the consumer society? Certainly, somehow. But I was convinced that not much humour was to be found here – humour seems to be alien to the public. No – an attack on the consumer society in the DDR is a joke in itself. What could one put in such a shopping basket? So I have to respect the citizens and comrades in the DDR: they have been steadfast in a difficult period, and there are many good features in the character of the DDR which an outsider must admire. The good lunch in Zurich, in the Garden Restaurant with a view over the whole city, would have fed a family in East Berlin for at least a day.

Basle keeps appearing as part of my journey towards reconciliation. In my Wuppertal lectures I often quoted from the works of Ekkehard Stegemann, admirable journeys of discovery into the world of the Bible and the theology of reconciliation. My colleague Heinrich Ott also lives in Basle. We have long talked about the concept of the fellow human being which he often uses in his writings, under the influence of Buber. But that brings us to another meeting, to an evening conversation in Basle.

Evelyn and I were back in Basle. Ekkehard Stegemann had refused to reserve a hotel room for us – plenty of students were on vacation and had left rooms free for us in the student hostel, and we were to have meals with him. He had also invited Ott, whom I had not seen for years. We had once had an exciting trip together: the American army had the strange idea of sending three wise men to the Army chaplains in Germany: a Catholic, Professor R.A.F.Mackenzie; a Protestant, Professor Heinrich Ott, Karl Barth's successor in Basle; and a rabbi, me, the Director of the Leo Baeck College.

We got on well with one another, occasionally quarrelled in front of our astounded hearers, immediately became reconciled after the lectures, and each knew the weaknesses and the insuperable main arguments of the others. We enjoyed this 'rainbow coalition' very much. One thing particularly pleased me. In order to get the best rooms in the Army hotels, we needed a rank: we were all three generals (I think the civil rank was GS 16). I sat in a car flying a flag with stars at the front, and everyone saluted automatically – until they saw me, and then hesitated. Something wasn't quite right.

Now I would be seeing Heinrich Ott again.

'What's he doing now?' I asked Ekkehard.

'He's a general,' he said – he knew the story.

But it was true. He now had the highest rank as chaplain in the Swiss Army and was very active in this and similar areas. I regretted this, because he had so much to offer in theology, but had to concede that he had already done an extraordinary amount there as a young man. He too was writing a multi-volume Church Dogmatics, and he was expanding the world of encounter between Christianity and other religions. He still had his chair in Basle, but his military duties were involving him more deeply in politics. This evening, in Ekkehard's house, he could rest from these things. Here he was again in the realm of theology. Ekkehard Stegemann had come to Basle from Heidelberg and introduced many new ideas to his new university. It seemed to me that he had overcome the initial difficulties – but who can judge that from outside? Swiss faculties, above all theological faculties, are quite conservative. A careful, thorough scholar like Stegemann was well suited to bringing fresh air into this atmosphere.

It was beautiful on the balcony. The wine bottles slowly emptied, and the stars seemed near enough to touch. I wanted to hear more about Ott's ideas about fellow human beings, but the stars seemed to fascinate him. We spoke about space travel. A very orthodox rabbi of my acquaintance once expressed his concern as to how a Jewish space-traveller could say his prayers on the moon: if the day is so short, he would really have to race from one prayer to another. (The halachic response is that one follows the rite in Jerusalem.) Ott went on to talk about other things, about the possibilities of life on other planets. I told him Arthur Clarke's story 'The Star'. A spaceship from earth comes to a distant galaxy and finds the remnants of a star which exploded a long time previously as a nova. The remnants attest that there had been a far greater and better civilization there than on earth. The priest astronaut in the spaceship calculates and establishes that the star became a nova, i.e. for a short time the brightest star in the sky, at the time of Jesus' birth. It was the star of Bethlehem. Clarke leaves it to readers to draw the consequences and moral for themselves. It became a little close on the balcony...

I believe that there are other worlds where people live, where God has revealed himself, and this is a certain consolation for me. I cannot get out of this post-Auschwitz world, and only have the hope and confidence that my life will continue after death – but I do not know how. And I keep thinking of the worlds which have been destroyed by human beings – a million Jewish children in the camps and all the others who died in concentration camps: Jews, Sinti, homosexuals, Communists, Social Democrats, Christians. Each person is a complete world in himself or herself. Heinrich Ott kept on with his thoughts about the distant planets, the possibilities there. Was there another elect people there? How else could revelation show itself? Ekkehard did not enjoy this topic very much. And it was indeed only a nocturnal conversation, like a dream which disappears in the light of day.

Other nocturnal conversations, dark thoughts, pursued me during an evening walk through empty streets. Ghosts came and talked to me. Was I in Basle? In Zurich, in New York or Berlin? My dead teacher and friend Jakob Taubes appeared in my thoughts and we mourned together. His father had been a rabbi in this land, and it was said that he committed suicide. I don't know – it need not be true – but his father died young. A cruel destiny ruled over the family. Jacob's wife Susan committed suicide, his cousin Uriel Tal (Taubes) shot himself, and there were other blows of fate. Deep sorrow overwhelmed him, and often the inner divide became too much for him. Buber called Taubes the most brilliant man of his time, but one who was his own enemy and destroyed himself... Taubes was not just one of my PhD supervisors; he also introduced me to the world of the students, in the revolution of 1968. I sat in his room in Berlin and watched him: on one telephone he was talking to the mayor, and on the other he was in conversation with Rudi Dutschke. He was trying to reach a compromise, he wanted to avoid confrontation, but didn't succeed. Taubes and Gollwitzer had published a joint letter addressed to the students and to the government. He warned against using the students as scapegoats. The breaking of the windows at Springer Verlag was not to be described as 'the new Kristallnacht'; the students were not Nazis.

I saw Taubes for the last time shortly after the death of our friend Arthur Cohen, who had died young of cancer. 'Death is waiting for me, it's coming soon,' he said. I deeply regret that I didn't take this seriously. I thought that it was his melancholy again, promised to write to him soon – and suddenly received news of his death. Cancer had caught up with him in Berlin, and I mourned deeply. That night in Basle I thought of death, friendly death that one cannot escape in Samarkand, that always stands by the wayside and waves... even when one has escaped the darkest time, indeed precisely then. Many of the great writers who found their way through the time of the Holocaust died early. Many met with death. Holbein's pictures in Basle also show death waiting. Did he know that death stood in his way – not in Basle, where his wife and children lived, but in London? I doubt it. His death came so quickly, so unexpectedly. In the time of the Black Death there were two solutions. One segregated the sick in a kind of camp, or one put oneself along with other healthy people in a kind of fortress, and that was also a camp. Then one sought a scapegoat: illness and death had to be the result of sin, perhaps original sin. 'The Jews have poisoned the wells,' went the saying. And so my ancestors died.

I wandered further through the quiet streets of Basle, on my way into the past. Almost half a century has passed since the Nazi period used the scapegoat theme so industriously. Old and new antisemites had been only to ready to recognize it as public policy and life-style. Many were not convinced, but they kept quiet. Nevertheless, the theme of the scapegoat is more than a curiosity of past times. It keeps cropping up when society is in crisis – it is too tempting to foist the guilt on others and to believe that that solves the problem.

We have a crisis, and we have a scapegoat. One could call the crisis the Black Death, although people want to avoid this identification. Aids is a plague. And the scapegoats are homosexuals. The Middle Ages and its solutions are practised again. Segregation. No contact, no touching. Disease comes from sin and the sufferers must be punished. Much in this reaction is flight from friendly death, the attempt to build a fortress of healthy people into which death cannot creep. But one cannot live in isolation.

Night thoughts in Basle.

And then comes the morning, which affirms life and fellow human beings.

8, 9, 10 November 1988:
After the Night

I know that the word 'Kristallnacht' trivializes the pogrom night, conceals the dead behind the broken glass from the windows and chandeliers, turns the history of murder into a crude but understandable action in the streets. Nevertheless the word 'Kristallnacht' remains in my memory: it describes my experiences over those days and nights, the glass under my feet, the wild chase, the hiding place, the lucky escape, and the rescue. I feel obligated to take part in the ceremonies commemorating it. But this brought problems in 1988: I cannot be in three places at the same time, and so I had to decide, where would I be on 9 November?

I so wanted to be in New York. *Kaddish for Terezin*, with music by Ronald Senator and libretto by me, was to be performed in America on 8 November, in a programme in memory of Kristallnacht. But I had promised my friends in Germany to be with them over those days, and I had to keep this promise. Evelyn went to New York. Because she wanted to speak in a variety of congregations (about 'Kristallnacht' and her work in saving the small village synagogues in Germany) she arranged things so that she could be there at the premiere. It was an unforgettable experience for her, and even the critics spoke in praise of this religious cantata.

And I was on the way to Hamburg. Hamburg? One has in the end to try to do as much as possible with the few rabbis who live in Germany. The whole world was in Berlin. So I went to Hamburg. In London, in New York and in many other countries the congregations were agreed: on the night of 9 November all the lights in the synagogues would cast their light through the windows; the world was to understand that the 'eternal light' in the synagogues cannot be quenched. We would not forget the attack on the houses of God, and in Hamburg and Berlin I wanted to remind others of that.

Hamburg. I often see Hamburg through Heine's poems, and therefore have mixed feelings about it – but this time I did not succumb to the temptation to quote from his poems or letters. A taxi took me to the Catholic Academy. I was offered a light meal, but I could hardly eat. There in the dining room, on all the walls, I was addressed by all the topics that I had been discussing with an ecologist on the plane. Now it was Sister Paula who was speaking to me, formerly Tisa, Countess of Schulenburg. The pictures, bronze and aluminium works dealt with the theme of the persecution of the Jews; the way into the camp, the women of Auschwitz, the children of the Warsaw ghetto... it was almost too much. The best sketch was perhaps the 'burning synagogue on Kristallnacht', but I stayed a particularly long time in front of three sketches: 'Jean Amery', 'O you chimneys' (Nelly Sachs) and 'Glory of Ashes' (Paul Celan). I bought some, and also her autobiography. Soon afterwards I got a letter from from Sister Paula, who wrote a good deal to me about her thoughts after 1933. On this 8 November she gave me courage and a deeper understanding of the work that now faced me.

It was the evening of 8 November. My friends in Hamburg had prepared everything carefully. Monsignor Sanders had made my stay in the Academy a real joy through his hospitality, and many colleagues took me to the 'Michel', the great church where my dialogue partner was already waiting for me. Paul Oestreicher and I were to repeat this dialogue the next evening in East Berlin. Our meeting in Hamburg was a prelude, a preparation. My real partner in Hamburg was Martin Stöhr, with whom I have worked so often that he knows me well. That is important. He knows what to expect of me; he accompanies me to the town, to the place, tells me the topic, about which he has already written twice, and then hopes for the best.

Around the Michel there used to be many Jewish homes, which have all disappeared. On the way to the Academy my taxi took me past the 'New Israelite Hospital'; the driver didn't know it. What is still left? A little, as I learned the next day. But this evening I experienced something of the regret, the pain and the memory that are alive in the Christian community. What I said and what my Christian partner said was received by the great congregation in profound silence. Then there were questions, without answers. No answers to the questions, but we stayed together informally so as not to go out into the cold night. When our small group sat in the restaurant afterwards, we returned to our dialogue proper with old and new friends. But I was pensive: shouldn't I be sitting this evening with the Jews of Hamburg, with those who are 'my own'? A story occurred to me.

The Jehudi was asked: 'The Talmud explains that the stork is called *chassida*, the pious one, the loving one, in Hebrew, because it shows love to its own. So why is it then counted among the unclean birds?' He gave the answer: 'Because it shows love only to its own.'

But the next day I was with my own – Pastor Keller took me to the site of the former synagogue which today, 9 November, was being dedicated as a memorial and centre for the history of Hamburg. I sat in the front row, alongside Rabbi Levinson (we were fellow students in Cincinnati) and we heard many good speeches about this past. Finally Peter Levinson spoke, and his speech was applauded loudly. Peter simply said, 'You've been standing here in the freezing cold for hours. The speeches are going to be printed – I'll spare you mine.'

Then he spoke a short prayer and left the rostrum. This was certainly the best speech, the most humane. But it had also been important to hear the others: contemporary eye-witnesses, politicians, clergy, and also the cantor with the prayer for the dead. Only when the people went away from the place and it was empty again could I see the lines which were engraved there: the star of David, the recollection of the past, and of former fellow-citizens. Some people were talking at this time about 'Kristallnacht' – but the place still remained empty. A synagogue would never stand here again. Or?

Then we drove to the synod, my real host in Hamburg. Here Martin Stöhr and I were to engage in dialogue with the group. It is always strange to come into such a group. One meets very open, enlightened people, and also the opposite. I always have to remind myself that people who think rigidly, people who hang on to their prejudices grimly, who build their religious thought on stony dogmas, need not necessarily be bad. They are sorry to say 'no' to others, but they believe they have no choice. And so it sometimes (though rarely) happens that our theme of Jews and Christians, election and witnesses to God, the one way and the many ways to God, will be attacked. Usually one need not answer oneself – and here other people in the synod spoke for us. And the great majority were on our side, were aware that on 9 November a work of repentance and confession had to be done, and that is why a rabbi had come to them. Martin and I could have spoken far longer, but I had to remember that a plane to Berlin awaited me, for my dialogue in the Sophienkirche was to begin at 7.30 that evening. And so I left again, in the car. Traffic jam. More traffic jams. Great uncertainty whether I would make it, and no time to reflect on the important moments of the meeting. Had something changed in my hearers? In myself? What had I learned, what had I taught?

I was the last on the plane. A restless flight, nothing to eat, and growing unrest. One can travel too much and say too little. One really must have time to meet one's audience after a paper, to understand what has happened. One must also have time for oneself, time to observe one's own journey. But now I was on the way to Berlin, where I had experienced 'Kristallnacht' fifty years earlier.

Berlin.

We landed at Tegel at 7 p.m. Fabulous – in half an hour I was to speak in East Berlin. But this time I was well prepared. Jon Greenwald is now in charge of the political section of the embassy, and he was my 'Jehu', my chauffeur. I found that this made crossing Checkpoint Charlie easier, and I arrived at the Sophienkirche in time. They had already begun: slides, short dramatic scenes performed by students, and loud music. It was a 'happening', above all for the young people. Two thousand were in the church and hundreds were standing outside and listening to the whole thing over loudspeakers. The canon and the rabbi were already known from previous visits. But this time it was different, for the students and also for us.

Much had already happened over the past two days. The government, the Jewish community and many representatives of Jews throughout the world had commemorated the past in a variety of events. On the evening of 9 November most of the Jewish guests were at the theatre for 'Nathan the Wise'. But the students and many Christians came to us. We sat there opposite one another, Paul and I, and spoke about the experiences of our youth fifty years ago. Paul, walking hand in hand with his mother, must have worn a magic hat, so that he could observe many things without people being suspicious of him. I myself ran like a hunted beast through the streets – I had to find the way back into hiding, deny my identity, run through the broken glass. The congregation listened to our conversation again in complete silence, as in Hamburg the evening before. But it was quite different. This time Paul and I were experiencing the past again, with anxiety and a beating heart. And even more than in Hamburg we also felt what was happening in the audience. They were becoming part of the event, were taking part in the past at this moment, were with us and not on the side of the hunters. When this service without prayer, with Jews and Christians, without liturgy but in a church, came to an end and the people left the church, the congregation became a torchlight procession, which went to a place commemorating the deportations, also to pray and remember there.

I went home, to Jon Greenwald and his parents from Wilkes Barre, where I had once been their rabbi. On the morning of 10 November we went to the consecration of the foundation stone of the synagogue in Oranienburgerstrasse, which is now to be rebuilt and to become a museum and school. I met the whole American delegation and of course also the English group. Jon had brought his camera and I was again able to test out the gaps in the security procedures. I was allowed to go into the front row, to talk with the Russian and the English ambassador (all credit to the Englishman, who translated the Russian into English and vice versa without a moment's hesitation). Jon with his camera walked through all the barriers without any difficulty. When the Mayor and Herr Honecker came, he climbed on to the stand with the television journalist and photographers, who cursed him loudly and openly because the stand shook and all their pictures suffered. In the evening he showed me his film. Of course I found most amusing the moment when Honecker shook my hand. He looked somewhat offended, as though he were well aware that Friedlander should not really be being given the hand of Comrade Honecker and was simply standing in for Rabbi Schindler, who was ill. When all was said and done I hadn't any decorations – not even the decoration awarded to Alex Schindler – to bring him. But I must say that I was nevertheless impressed by the event. Erich Honecker was in a concentration camp for ten years, and his understanding for the suffering of the prisoners arose out of his own experience. Although one cannot speak of a 'reparation', it is notable that the government showed a lively interest in the Jewish community and gave it much support. More happened in the Federal Republic, and it was only the unhappy Jenninger speech which overshadowed the achievements in Bonn.

A word about that. Now we have sufficient detachment to see the decency of the man again. That does not mean that I have changed the opinion which I expressed in an interview with *Der Spiegel*: an almost criminal folly must be punished. On this day Herr Jenninger had refused to allow Jewish representatives to speak in the Bundestag. He wanted to speak himself. I assume that he saw this as his duty, and so he let no one edit his speech. When one reads the speech today it is in part a quite objective description of the feelings and thoughts which dominated Germans during the Hitler period. But the frightful quotations were spoken so unfeelingly – he did not dissociate himself from them, either by his tone or by the addition of his own words, which would have made it clear that this was a report, and was not being assented to. One of the English newspapers produced an apt comparison: it was like a funeral for a murdered child. A prominent figure gives a funeral speech. Coolly, without excitement, he talks about the psyche, about the mental illnesses and inhibitions of the murderer, which made this murder possible. And this is heard as a defence – no word of compassion, of mourning, nothing about the loss which the whole world has suffered through this murder. I recently saw Fritz Lang's film M again. The child murderer (Peter Lorre) defends himself at the end of the film and shows why he was helpless against the demon that had him in its grip. Lorre defends himself with passion and pathos, and he expresses his horror about himself. Herr Jenninger lacked precisely this passion: 'He was out for lunch,' as they say in America. Something was missing in him when he made this speech; he was not aware how much grief he caused his upright colleagues in the Bundestag.

Conor Cruise O'Brien, an honest voice in England, protested against Jenninger's fall: 'A man is being punished for speaking the truth'. He assumed that those who left the chamber in protest had been German nationalists who saw the honour of the German people attacked. 'Here their former anti-Jewish convictions were being pilloried, and they wanted to escape Jenninger's accusations,' he said. What a misunderstanding! Had Conor Cruise O'Brien seen the television broadcast, the weeping faces of the audience, had he read out the roll of honour of those who left – Frau Hamm-Brücher and many fighters against antisemitism of yesterday and today – he would not have expressed his opinion like this. He was right to defend Herr Jenninger against the charge of antisemitism, but the folly and the lack of feeling remain. Jenninger was not a scapegoat who was punished for the sins of others; he made his own mistake. I hope that he finds the way back to political work; it would be sad to see in the wilderness an embittered man who has done good service in the past.

Where was I? Oh yes, in East Berlin, on 10 November. Somehow I had become part of the American delegation, in a car which now took me from Oranienburgerstrasse to the new Centre for the Study of Judaism. More speeches from the Jewish and the state side. Then an enormous buffet (it is remarkable how I always end up eating). And there was a conversation with a member of the government whom I do not want to identify more closely.

'Was it really necessary,' I asked him, 'for the Jewish speakers to praise the state so much? We know how good things are for the Jews in the DDR, how the state protects them and gives them rights. But when one keeps hearing it, the remarks lose their force.'

'What can one do?,' he said. 'We have freedom of speech here. No one is told what to say. They *wanted* to say that. And I can tell you that the last speaker had five further paeans of praise in his speech which we deleted.'

One can only pay ironic respect to this kind of freedom of the press.

The cars drove on. Our American Reform group wanted to honour the 'birthplace' of Jewish science and so we went to Tucholskystrasse (formerly Artilleriestrasse). 'Who was Tucholsky?' some people asked. I explained that this poet could not be regarded as the founder of Jewish letters, but that he had many connections with Heinrich Heine... 'Who was...?' Now at any rate we were standing in front of a house in which the College of the Study of Judaism, the school for Reform rabbis, once was. The memorial plate hangs by the door, and it is important for us to come here as a confirmation of our own identity. Leo Baeck's granddaughter, Marianne Dreyfus, spoke for the group, and I gave a short explanation which introduced something of the history and development of Reform Judaism into this time of prayer and remembrance. Only a few minutes from here there once stood Esriel Hildesheimer's school for Orthodox rabbis – but in reality the two schools were miles apart; the distance between them was unbridgable. At this time of remembrance I felt a special grief, a deep sorrow: the past with its conflicts and contradictions determines the present. What will the future be? More division or a coming together of Orthodox and Liberals? Here too there must be interconfessional dialogue. Not through reason, as is often thought, but through the passion of love which compels all things. Martin Buber tells this story:

> From his youth up, Rabbi Moshe Teitelbaum was an enemy of Hasidic teaching, since it seemed to him to be – heresy. He once visited his friend, Rabbi Joseph Asher, who was also an enemy of Hasidism. In those days the prayer book of Master Luria, whose word is an ancestor of the Hasidic word, had just been printed. When it was brought to these

two rabbis, Rabbi Moshe snatched the heavy book from the messenger and threw it on the ground. Rabbi Josef Asher picked it up and said: 'But it is a prayer book, and one must not show contempt for it.'

When this incident was reported to the Lubliner (Rabbi Jaakob Jizhak), he said: 'Rabbi Moshe will become a Hasid. Rabbi Joseph Asher will remain an opponent. For the one who has the great blaze of hostility can burn for God, but the one whose aversion is cold has the way closed to him.' And so it was.

Something about this story disturbs me. I seldom show the passion of Moshe Teitelbaum. In my first congregation in Fort Smith, Arkansas, I was the successor of a Rabbi Moshay Teitelbaum. Everyone said: Teitelbaum and Friedlander are like day and night. I was a 'Jecke', a thoughtful German Jew. Will I therefore always remain remote from charismatic religion? And my hating, loving opponents: they are only waiting for me to join them.

Berlin, 10 November. Events now run together. I know that I and others visited the English and American ambassadors. They were alike in their enthusiasm and their understanding for the situation – and I no longer know whether it was the Englishman or the American who spoke such good Russian. At all events, these visits lie under the seal of state secrecy (which means that I've really forgotten what was said). And I also somehow still had time to visit the Humboldt University to study the Jewish prayer book, the Siddur, with a large group of students. As usual they had invited two foreign scholars (as we were all in East Berlin) to be sure of at least one of them. Somewhat unexpectedly, I appeared at the right time. I came from London, Michael Krupp from Jerusalem. And the introduction to the Jewish prayer book became a Jewish-Christian dialogue which brought us nearer to one another. The rhythm of the prayers, the development of ideas which made us a bridge ascending between human beings and God, the language of love which brought us from the liturgy to the Bible, above all to the Song of Songs, all this was quite unexpected for me. I almost forgot that there were still students sitting in front of us, who occasionally asked a question. So it became a real dialogue. We had not planned any particular agenda, were not there to proclaim apologetic or enlightening thoughts. We were talking about a book, a prayer book that we both love. It was one of the most important hours for me on this visit to East Berlin.

Next day I flew back to London, to my rather lonely home. Evelyn was also occupied with memories of the pogrom night, but in America. Before she went, she had recorded a broadcast for the German service of the BBC which I – of course – thought the best thing that the BBC had on offer at that time. She had been given a tape recorder, and she visited various villages in Bavaria, in southern Germany, to ask older people, 'Where were you on Kristallnacht?' There were some shattering answers. Her mother, her aunt and I were voices on the tape. After that she used research material from the Wiener Library in London: the reports of the English Ambassador in Berlin, the debates in Parliament ('Can you tell us that everything possible is being done for the sufferers in Germany?' 'I can assure you that all necessary steps will be taken – a commission is being appointed to investigate the facts'). Newspaper commentaries from November 1938 provided many quotations. This produced a broadcast which showed the excitement and the sympathy, but also the cold rejection of Jewish suffering. The programme was also used by a German station. I am proud of Evelyn's work and grateful for it.

Now we are working together for the future: conferences in Loccum, in Aachen, in Neuwied, preparations for the Berlin Kirchentag, and we are still under the spell of the past which cannot become future. How far have we come on our journey towards reconciliation? How far have the others come? And the world?

One day, after the destruction of the Temple, the disciples of the rabbis were walking with their pupils near the Temple. And they were weeping. 'When will redemption come?', they asked. Their teachers answered: 'The question always comes in the dark of night, when redemption seems impossible – it will never get light again. But then comes the dawn, first slowly, a white line on the horizon, and then, suddenly, a thread of gold. And with the first rays of the sun the darkness is banished. So it is with redemption. It begins slowly, almost imperceptibly, but then it comes faster and faster, and suddenly the whole world is in bright light.'

This can also happen between people, in the sphere of reconciliation. But that is not the same thing as redemption. We remain unredeemed. New acts of cruelty stand between us and the light. Every day people are destroyed, near to us and far away. Precisely for that reason we must find the way to one another, in order not to leave victory to the darkness. The way goes through our own identity, our own reconciliation and recognition of the Holy that will pave our way to freedom. There we meet our fellow men and women, and through our fellow men and women we find the way to God.

The encounters which I have described here were signposts for me towards reconciliation. Now I must travel on. Robert Frost's poem remains as a motto:

> But I have promises to keep
> and miles to go before I sleep
> and miles to go before I sleep.

And the Wall Came
Tumbling Down

'And miles to go before I sleep'

It might have been wiser to conclude the previous chapter with a different poem by Robert Frost, to end with his observation that 'good fences make good neighbors'. On 9 November 1989 Evelyn and I were in Toledo, the city of Don Quixote and of Don Juan, of El Greco (who lived in Samuel Halevi's house) and Moses ibn Ezra. We were not there as tourists, but had come to a scholarly conference in order to deliver papers. Evelyn lectured on the *genizot* (hiding places for damaged Jewish texts) in Bavarian village synagogues, and I spoke about Leo Baeck in the concentration camp. In time-honoured fashion, the scholars milled around in the conference hall and sipped the local sherry; for a change, I was not the first at the table.

Weeping, I sat in our hotel room upstairs, in front of the television set. The direct German broadcast from Berlin was transmitting the fall of the Wall. Young men were bicycling along the top of the Wall, and a stream of men, women and children were surging through all the openings of what had been an iron curtain between East and West Berlin. The 'thread of gold' on the horizon had turned into the sunlight of freedom, and I half expected to hear the sound of the prisoners' march from Beethoven's *Fidelio* as East Berlin propelled itself into the West.

The East Berliners who came that day wandered about as though in a daze, experiencing all the emotions of released prisoners clutching an unexpected pardon in their hands. Wide-eyed, they wandered through the streets of West Berlin, examining the realities of the 'good life' they had previously seen only on television and dismissed as propaganda. Many of them planned to stay in West Germany, but the majority went back to East Berlin, sometimes travelling back and forth to assure themselves that they could leave the DDR any time they chose to do so. In the months that followed, I could observe fascinating new developments in East and West Germany. For example, there were the little Trabants (poor relatives in East Germany pretending to be Volkswagens). Rickety, air-polluting and noisy, they streamed across the border. At first they were welcomed. Later, when West Berlin became a vast car park for them, they were sometimes vandalized – but they have also become status symbols for wealthy young West Germans across the land! And the early euphoria soon gave way to doubts and misgivings. Meanwhile, at this moment, there was a universal rejoicing at a freedom experienced on so visible a level, a freedom which arrived in so unexpected a fashion.

But was it that unexpected? The previous September, I had a strange and almost traumatic encounter with some Germans of the type I had basically avoided in my travels through Germany. A television producer had asked me to join in a discussion on the future of Germany, fifty years after the beginning of World War II (this was in September 1989). The Channel 4 'After Dark' show is an unstructured and open-ended dialogue programme which starts around midnight and ends about three hours later. I was asked to join Christof Wackenagel, a former Baader-Meinhof actor and poet who had been released from prison after serving time for shooting a policeman – but who had reformed! Then there was a Herr Spitzi from Austria who was a 'revisionist' historian and questioned whether a Holocaust had in fact happened; a camp survivor; a *Wall Street Journal* writer; a psychiatrist; and Franz Schoenhuber, head of the new Republican Party in Germany. At the last election, this extreme right-wing party had gathered over ten per cent of the German vote, and Franz Schoenhuber had won a seat in the European Parliament; some still felt that he might be the coming 'Führer' of a new 'Fourth Reich'. It must be said that Schoenhuber will take anyone to court who

137

applies the term 'Nazi' to him; and in the programme, he recognized and condemned the crimes of the Nazis. Nevertheless, all right-wing groups in Germany would vote for him and support him.

Could I sit down with such people and talk with them? The openness I had claimed for myself throughout my German sojourn was put to a test now; and I felt I had to take part in the programme. At least three times during the long night I excused myself and marched out of the TV studio, into the street, to breathe fresh air (I also went to the toilet, realizing for the first time that the Bible is right: the kidneys are a seat for the human emotions). Franz Schoenhuber insisted, throughout the discussions, that a 'reunification' of Germany had to take place, that it would lead to a redrawing of the Polish border, and that all this would happen quickly – and no one in the room believed him. But the real pressure upon me came from Herr Spitzi. That gentleman had had a great war, working first with Ribbentrop, and in the Secret Service run by Canaris – but, of course, he only heard about the concentration camps after the war, at the Nuremberg trials! 'Oh, sure, we joked about Dachau in our office,' he shared with us. 'If you don't behave, you'll get there!' But death camps? Goodness, no. Goebbels really wanted peace; Goering had been a prince of a fellow. And Spitzi himself had been honoured when Hitler marched into Vienna. The war itself had been a big poker game and Germany was just outbluffed by the Allies – a real pity! He also seemed to suggest a good relationship between himself and Chancellor Waldheim. And I was sick sitting next to him. He was the German past. Was Schoenhuber the future?

Half a year later that fear has receded. After the May elections, when his party failed dismally, Schoenhuber resigned as head of the Republican party. Later, he regained control, but remains unimportant. Schoenhuber's programme on unification was shared to some extent by all other political groups in Germany, and he did not have much else to offer. Perhaps that is why, during his final months in office, he joined LePen in France in a public programme which suggested their shared ideals. But I am still frightened of him, partly for a very personal reason: the man was very likeable; a certain charisma surrounded him. In a strange way we were drawn to each other, and he gave me his private number in Munich before he left the TV studio. (I tore it up five minutes later. Still, five minutes...) And his stance of admitting what happened under the Nazis and then distancing himself from it: 'but that was fifty years ago... we are the new Germany, innocent of that past which is not ours... but proud to be Germans...' *That* could be a pattern for others. On TV, Wackenagel kept shouting at him and Spitzi, 'But aren't you ashamed? How can you live as Germans and not be ashamed?', and Schoenhuber put him down by genially asking about his crimes against the German state. As for Franz Schoenhuber's war record: 'I was a young sergeant in the Waffen SS, only a soldier doing his duty' – that was a past which no longer mattered. And of course, people can change. Wackenagel had changed.

A dialogue does not only take place among friends; one can and does encounter enemies, generally in a framework where they have undeniable rights and privileges. But I am not as good a person as my late friend the poet Erich Fried, who could and did sit down with former Nazis and turn them into friends. I can feel and appreciate humaneness and the humane in others whom I distrust instinctively, and whose record makes them suspect to me. I cannot be comfortable with them. We often work for a common cause alongside people we dislike; and often the cause will bring us together, and we learn to appreciate the other person. Perhaps we do not need a structure – but simply being human should be enough. I often think of the shortest, ultimate science-fiction horror story: 'The last person in the world was seated in a room. There was a knock at the door.' I could not live in a world without other humans: Judaism does not appreciate the hermit's life, the withdrawal from the ebb and flow, the interplay of human lives through which we move towards the dimension of God. Even then, there is such loneliness; such utter loneliness. The occasional encounters with others, even the encounter with God, come to emphasize the long stretches of solitude which make up the bulk of our lives. We live in exile; and we die alone. But at the horizon of our existence there is a gleam called hope.

It may well be that the two Germanies came together out of

sheer loneliness. They had been a pariah people, an outcry among the nations. And then, East Germany had found a cover called Communism. The Communists had fought against the Nazis. Honecker had been a concentration camp prisoner for ten years – obviously, every German Nazi lived in West Germany. An East German concentration camp museum, as its last exhibit, offered a shield with an arrow: 'The way continues, to Bonn!' And so, the East Germans had not come to terms with their past. They had not confessed. They had not mourned. No attempt of any scope had been made to pay restitution to the victims of the past: '...go to the West Germans!' In just the same way, they had been eyeing West Germany with mixed love and hatred. The 'economic miracle' had been viewed with envy, had been balanced by their stress upon the fact that no one had helped East Germany, that they were creating a caring society in which they shared the little that they did possess. And this was true. Throughout my visits to East Germany I had been impressed by this aspect of a socialist state in which, apparently, the little that it possesed was shared. And then the cover was blown. The concealed corruption came out into the open and the people came to realize that they had not only been brainwashed about the situation in West Germany – they had been betrayed by their own leaders, and by their own neighbours.

The 'Stasis' – the State Security System – had been a state within a state, paying over a hundred thousand employees to spy on the rest. In 1988 I had lectured in Halle, in a private home to friends, so that I did not have to be registered officially, or to apply for permission to speak which would not be granted. It had been a good visit. Now, in 1990, my friends pointed out that the house next door had been a Stasi centre, that microphones had recorded every word I had spoken, that photographs existed of everyone who had entered the building! And what I had said had been so innocuous – but it all helped to support the 'spy industry'. The East Germans had been released from that system, and a great burden had been taken from them. But a different burden had been placed upon their shoulders.

'Wir stehen im Jahr Null – we're in the Year Zero – just as in

1945,' said a Catholic priest from Halle to me. 'And we have a double burden to carry.'

For a long time, Father Heinrich Pera had tried to establish a hospice movement in the DDR, had visited Dame Cecily Saunders in Great Britain to learn from her and others, and had been frustrated by the establishment. Now, he hopes to see something established. But he also serves a congregation, and tried to confront them, in his church in Halle, with the immediate past, in which they could not claim to have been innocent of the crimes which are now being uncovered: not only the use of the old Nazi concentration camps to kill opponents of Communism, but also the daily acceptance and acquiescence which had involved all of them in the suppressing of human rights. 'You have not yet mourned; you have not wept, you have not confessed, you have not wept!' he told them from the pulpit. And people stood up in the pews to scream at him, accusing him of travelling along with the state and of not speaking out loudly enough. 'You didn't lead us properly,' they said to him. Perhaps this was part of the traditional pattern of seeking out scapegoats, of finding someone to blame in order to free themselves of their guilt. Certainly the Stasis, the Poles ('coming in here as black marketeers') and even the Jews were being viewed as scapegoats upon whom the sins of the nation could be placed. The guilt of the Nazi period, of the Communist regime – all of it was being pushed away, was being suppressed. Now, one just wanted to be a German: a good, decent well-to-do German in the pattern of Helmut Kohl. 'We are not what we were; we are what we will be' – the middle German with the power of a rich technocracy.

During Christmas 1989 the East German ambassador in Great Britain invited a group of Berlin Jews to the Embassy. Evelyn and I accepted. Arriving at a fashionable late time to what we felt would be a huge reception, we were met with the hurt look accorded to chief guests who keep the others waiting: only twenty-five guests were present. Dr Mitdank, the ambassador, immediately launched into his major speech, in which he showed himself a most liberal statesman who had always condemned the personality cult of Honecker. I responded with great courtesy, but also pointed to the new worries of a Jewish community which saw outbreaks of anti-semitism in East Germany and in Eastern Europe. We were assured that the fight against injustice would characterize the new Germany. Later, during the meal – unfortunately during a lull in the conversation when everyone was listening – I could not restrain my sense of humour. 'Dr Mitdank,' I said to the ambassador, 'did you know that I am a collector of fine art?' He gave me a perplexed look. 'Oh, yes,' I assured him, 'I collect portraits. I am certain you have a fine portrait of Honecker in the basement now which you would sell at a rock-bottom price.' There was a moment of dead silence, followed by laughter which built up into a respectable crescendo. Dr Mitdank has a fine diplomatic ear, and his laughter soon led all the rest. 'Take it,' he said to me; '*please* take it!' And it struck me how ready East Germany was to rid itself of its past. When the elections did come, a scandal in the pro-Kohl faction did not matter; able leadership of the 'reformed' Communist party did not count (although Herr Gisy was attacked as a 'Jewish pig' by extremists); the people simply voted on the principle of 'union now' and wanted nothing as much as giving up their independence and melting into West Germany. Plato's *Symposium* speaks of love and of marriage as the coming together of two halves of a whole who have been searching for each other throughout the world. Something like it happened in East Germany, although East Berlin was at odds with the rest of the DDR. But, like all relationships, it united many aspects; and hate was not absent from that love.

The hatred towards minority groups which is part of a strong nationalism will also be imported into West Germany. It need not be that virulent antisemitism which is now evidencing itself in the Soviet Union (released when the pressure from above was removed) and which evidenced itself in Estonia, the Ukraine and in the Balkans. The March 1990 Jewish Book Week in London featured a round-table discussion involving Lord Beloff, Professor Peter Pulzer from Oxford, Rabbi Julia Neuberger and me. Again, the total emphasis was upon what would happen in Germany now. The audience of mainly elderly Jews expressed total horror and fear at the thought of a strong Germany which might again initiate persecutions.

'They started two world wars, and now they will begin the next one,' seemed to be a central thought in the hall. The professor who suggested that Great Britain was not altogether blameless in this matter was greeted with hostility, and Rabbi Neuberger's idea of establishing personal links with Germans was clearly the thought of the next generation. My own comment about the greater dangers to be found in France and LePen was met with incomprehension; for this group Germany remained the pariah nation. A few months later, after the profanation of graves and a Jewish body in Carpentras, France, their attitude changed. And yet, perversely, I felt more hope because most of Paris followed Mitterand into the streets for a protest march. But that generation is on the wane, and for the contemporary world the approach of Professor Arno Mayer in the USA seems far more representative: the Holocaust was part of a Thirty Year War within the twentieth century, and can only be understood within the general framework.

In May 1989, in a BBC television discussion with Mayer, I could only express my admiration for his brilliant historical insights, but warned him that revisionists like David Irving were misusing them in an attempt to show that the Holocaust had not happened, that there were no gas chambers in Auschwitz, and that the great German crusade against Bolshevism merely engaged in a bit of extra cruelty as a means to an end. Professor Mayer recognizes and teaches all of the unique aspects of the Holocaust. And yet, as a theologian, I had to remind him that the simple attempt to understand this *'tremendum'* by placing it into a rational framework did relativize something which remains irrational and incomprehensible: absolute evil happened. Our world was changed. And neither the victims nor the perpetrators can walk away from it. That, to my mind, is the most tragic thing happening in East Germany: a people running away from a past which they have not begun to understand, for which they do not yet feel responsible – and that covers all the fifty years, which have scarred and maimed them.

In April 1990, just before Passover, I had been scheduled to speak in Dresden, Leipzig and Karl-Marx-Stadt. We cancelled the engagement at the last moment: I had too much to do –

and they were grateful not to have to deal with the past. Their thoughts were all for the future, including the municipal elections. During the days of darkness, they had braved the Stasis to assemble for talks on Judaism and on the Holocaust. Now, they have a different agenda. Nevertheless the dialogue continues. May is the Katholikentag in West Berlin, where three of my talks were scheduled within that huge religious event.

The day before speaking in Berlin, a reception was held in the Sternberg Centre in London, and Cardinal Basil Hume, the Archbishop of London, presented me with the Sternberg Medal, the award made annually by the Council for Christians and Jews for inter-faith work. In return, I had to give a lecture on 'The Joy and Anguish of Interfaith'. I had recently returned from Basle, where I had had the *chutzpah* to lecture on 'Karl Barth and the Concept of Nothingness' to his old university, its lecturers and students (the first question came from Markus Barth, his son!). This gave me the opportunity of discussing the pain of dialogue, the confrontation with darkness, the many failures and the rare triumphs. A faculty meeting of the Leo Baeck College followed, which I left after a while to catch my taxi to Heathrow and my plane to Berlin.

Everything was the same, and everything was different. Again, the US embassy car waited for me at the airport, with Jon and Gaby Greenwald ready to drive me to East Berlin. But we drove through a new checkpoint, with only a cursory glance at the special *Dienstvisum* which I had obtained at the London embassy. And the quietness of East Berlin at night was only a memory now. Once, when the stores closed, they had rolled up the sidewalks (remember Philadelphia in the 1950s?). Now, Unter den Linden bustled with night life, with people going to and fro under the Brandenburg Gate. On the plane, I had been reading Len Deighton's *Spy Line*, which centred on the problem of smuggling a double agent through or under the 'Wall'. Now, she could have strolled across in a bikini without a challenge. And where was the frightening Secret Police? The people had stormed those offices in November, and had taken away vanloads of files. A book had just been published, *But I Love All of You*, with extracts from these files. Jon showed me a page where one of the agents reported how he had 'followed Mr Greenwald, the head of the Political Section of the US Embassy. Mr Greenwald visited a polling station during the elections, examined the booths, and talked to the voters... but he obtained a permit,' he concluded sadly. Now, no one remembers ever having received a fee for preserving the state by reporting the actions of any neighbour or friend.

Discussions now centred upon economic issues. One could still see queues in the streets – in front of shops selling East German goods at less than twenty per cent of the former price. And, at 7.30 a.m., on my way to West Berlin, I saw long lines in front of every bank: next week, East German marks would be exchanged at the ratio of one for one for West German marks – only 5,000 marks; the rest would be exchanged at two for one. And everyone was getting his bank account into shape. Of course, there were other, fascinating issues: 500 Soviet Jews had just arrived in East Berlin, and problems of integration within the Jewish community are being confronted with good will and some hope. The arrival of a large group of Rumanian gypsies seems to be more of a problem, particularly when one considers that in both East and West Berlin a certain type of xenophobia seems to be arousing itself from its slumber...

On this trip, I had to return to West Berlin, to the Katholikentag. The organizers and co-lecturer were standing in the street, outside the SFB radio station, stopping random passers-by, asking them if they were the rabbi. The sheaf of notes in my hand acted like an electric beacon for them, and I was practically lifted up the steps and pushed on to the rostrum of the lecture hall. Many of those waiting for me were from East Berlin, and it was curious to see that the West Germans seemed more advanced in the Christian-Jewish dialogue – but it is unfair to generalize. It was an East German who confronted me after the lecture: 'We have sinned, and must confess our sins and atone,' she said to me. 'But – aren't the victims also guilty in a sense?', she asked, 'Must they not also confess their sins as well?' I looked at her with much sadness. 'What sins would you want the million to confess who died in the camps?' I asked her. 'Oh, I didn't mean them,' she stuttered as she backed away and disappeared into the crowd... I went away to give

my second lecture, to a thousand people, and my third, to
about fifty dedicated, open people who had come to the Jewish
Lehrhaus. The small confrontation had disturbed me. There is
still so much sickness in people... and, perhaps, in the city.
Will Berlin ever be Berlin again?

At times, a city can be like a museum, particularly East Berlin.
What one sees there, what happens, is quite real. But at times
the buildings seem to pose, and the people become actors
going through their paces to an audience. The past is recreated
in a way one would have liked it to have been; and the future
is given its self-fulfilling prophecy. Somehow it all brought me
back to Toledo, to the visit Evelyn and I paid to the museum
which was once the home of El Greco. Everything had been
set up the way it was in his day – as an atelier, a work room, a
living place. The American museum director walking with us
grew pale. 'I would be in prison if I tried to do this in
Washington,' he whispered in a voice filled with horror. We
were standing in the studio of the artist, with his great picture
of St Peter upon the easel, where it could be examined and
touched by tourists. Occasionally, a flash from a camera illumi-
nated the scene, and a wind was sweeping in from the open
window. Somewhere in the distance the guard was hastily
finishing his cigarette. It might all have been a clear depiction
of what once did happen here – and perhaps museums should
be transitory happenings. But it was the present destroying
the past; and this happens in many areas of contemporary life.
Films with concentration camp scenes; swastikas on most of
the thrillers screaming for attention on the bookstalls of airports
and railway stations – a past which cannot be understood is
turned into an entertainment. Poisoned ideologies enter into
politics, and theologies try to obscure guilt by making everyone
guilty.

'The Road goes ever on and on,' sings Tolkien's Bilbo, but
Stephen Hawking, another Cambridge don, shows us time
turning back upon itself. And so we always come back to
the past, to the dangers lurking in objects or ideas. Once,
Chernobyl meant something beautiful in Jewish life: a dynasty
of rabbinic teachers who gave light to the world. Now, it is a
place of darkness, still surrounded by an armed guard who try

to stay far enough away from the deadly radiations. But why is it guarded at all? A cautionary tale for our time: looters entered that camp and still try to get past the guard in order to steal – religious objects. Icons! These icons then came into the black market, and were illegally exported. *And they are still radioactive*, bringing the wasting sickness into the homes of the purchasers.

We take other things out of the past which are damaging. But any temptation to give sermons must be scotched ruthlessly. We also take joy out of the past, light memorial candles which celebrate not anguish but blessing, and meet one another in the joy of true encounters. Perhaps this will happen in Germany. And the thread of gold on the horizon may become a shining day. Kafka once wrote that the messiah would not come on the last day but on the day after that day, and every sunrise brings us closer to the messianic time.